Teaching STEM Outdoors

Other Redleaf Press Books by Patty Born Selly

Connecting Animals and Children in Early Childhood

Early Childhood Activities for a Greener Earth

TEACHING STEM Outdoors
Activities for Young Children

PATTY BORN SELLY

Redleaf Press®
www.redleafpress.org
800-423-8309

Published by Redleaf Press
10 Yorkton Court
St. Paul, MN 55117
www.redleafpress.org

First edition 2017
Cover design by Beth Berry Mackenzie
Cover photograph by iStock.com/omgimages
Interior design by Jim Handrigan and Douglas Schmitz
Typeset in Chaparral Pro and AS Full Life
Interior photos by Dani Porter Born, Annie Thoraldson, Megan Gessler, Jessica Ostrov, and the author
Printed in the United States of America
24 23 22 21 20 19 18 17   1 2 3 4 5 6 7 8

Library of Congress Cataloging-in-Publication Data
Names: Selly, Patty Born.
Title: Teaching STEM outdoors : activities for young children / Patty Born
    Selly.
Description: St. Paul, MN : Redleaf Press, 2017. | Includes bibliographical
    references.
Identifiers: LCCN 2016043210 (print) | LCCN 2017004091 (ebook) | ISBN
    9781605545028 (paperback) | ISBN 9781605545035 (ebook)
Subjects: LCSH: Science--Study and teaching (Early childhood)--Activity
    programs. | Outdoor education. | BISAC: EDUCATION / Preschool &
    Kindergarten. | EDUCATION / Curricula. | EDUCATION / Teaching Methods &
    Materials / Science & Technology. | EDUCATION / Elementary.
Classification: LCC LB1139.5.S35 S45 2017 (print) | LCC LB1139.5.S35 (ebook)
    | DDC 372.35/7--dc23
LC record available at https://lccn.loc.gov/2016043210

Printed on acid-free paper

Dominic, Lucy, and Julian:
for you, everything, always

Contents

Foreword

by David Sobel

YOU'RE THINKING, "Here's another new-fangled idea (sigh): *Teaching STEM Outdoors*. I'm having enough trouble trying to figure out how to teach STEM indoors! Now they want me to teach it outside amid the bugs, traffic, mud, and yuck."

But really, teaching STEM outside isn't a new idea. Rather, it's just the invigoration of an old idea, like walking to school, helping your neighbor, or eating straight from the garden. STEM is just a fancy name for making things, fixing things, and figuring things out. Look at the turn-of-the-twentieth-century *Scouting for Girls*, *Handbook for Boys*, and other old campcraft manuals: they're all about how to start fires with wet wood, how to tie knots, and how to build a shelter that will keep you warm and dry. These are examples of interesting science, technology, and engineering problems being solved outdoors with tools and simple materials. So when Patty Born Selly invites you to take your students outside to figure out why there's erosion on the edge of the parking lot, or why shadows are longer in the morning than at noon, think of it as reliving the good old days rather than experimenting with a new idea.

The nice thing is that in *Teaching STEM Outdoors*, Patty makes it easy for you. She knows getting kids outside can be challenging. Making sure everyone has sun protection and/or rainboots isn't always a walk in the park. And what about that child with sensory integration issues who can't stand touching dirt? Patty guides you step-by-step through understanding what STEM activities (she terms them, "STEM Starts") are and why they're important. Then she articulates the necessary logistics for getting students out the door. And once you're out, she's got a zillion (well, 122 really) ideas for how to get started on STEM. It's as easy as mud pie. She's realistic as well: after carefully articulating the best approach, she cautions, "Don't get stuck on the steps." I appreciate this balanced wisdom.

There are a couple of other things about Patty's guidance that makes this book both appealing and useful. First of all, she's been there. She hasn't just gleaned these activities from other people's books. She's been in the trenches (well, the ditches perhaps) and done these activities herself. There's a great conversation she collected that illustrates children encountering, and then trying to solve, a real engineering problem. She describes how several children are working in the sand area to make a castle with a moat. They are trying to make a bridge out of sand so their toy horses can get across the moat, but the bridge keeps collapsing. Listen to their conversation:

NICO: It needs to be stronger!

CHRISTOPHER: The horses are too heavy!

FAITH: It's not big enough for the horses. It needs to be sturdier.

Eventually, the children all agree the bridge itself needs to be stronger in order to keep from crumbling and to allow the horses to stand on it. And then they generate some practical engineering solutions.

MIRA: We got to get some pinecones or something to stack up there in the river [moat].

CHRISTOPHER: We need a branch, like a log or a stick to lay over it like a bridge.

This is exactly the kind of authentic, grounded-in-real-play-in-the-real-world problem solving we want to encourage in young children. It's these firsthand portraits that make the book accessible.

I also appreciate Patty's connected-to-nature language. She explains the central organizing principle of the book like this: "In the world of gardening, 'plant starts' are small seedlings that have been sown and are ready to be planted and take root, and these STEM starts that appear throughout the book are similar. They can serve as starting points for investigations that you and your students will engage in, and, like the roots of a plant, your shared engagement will grow deeper over time."

This analogy between starting plants and starting STEM investigations appeals to me. Patty is providing advice as well as giving you the freedom to see how things grow in the soil and climate of your own classroom and schoolyard.

Nature cements the new learning. That's the big idea in this book. Taking STEM outside means the STEM learning is going to be more solidly cemented in the children's bodies and brains. And this healthier approach to being outdoors together, to solving problems outdoors, and to asking emergent questions and then figuring out how to answer them leads to what Patty calls "a community of curiosity." I am hopeful this book will encourage you to create a community of curiosity both inside your classroom as well as out there on the schoolyard and in the neighborhood.

Acknowledgments

To DOMINIC, LUCY, AND JULIAN: thank you for being there. I couldn't have done this without your support and willingness to indulge "just one more." Thank you for supporting me, cheering me on, being patient with me, and never giving up on me, despite the many adventures we haven't yet had time to get to because of this book. It's finished; let's go.

I am grateful, humbled, and honored to work in an educational landscape with amazing people who are doing so much to reconnect our children to nature and harness their excitement about STEM. Because of you, and the work that you do, our future is bright. These children are going to take us places we could never imagine!

To my many colleagues and friends in the early childhood, elementary, and higher education world, I'm grateful beyond words for your support. This is an important time for children, nature, and STEM, and you incredible people are ushering in change with open arms. Your expertise, advice, feedback and ideas have contributed so much to this work—and I hope my contribution as well can be something useful and good. The fact that all of your names won't fit here is a testament to how many people I leaned on, called upon, and pestered with all my STEM and child development questions. I feel deep gratitude to you for so generously sharing your work, thoughts, feedback, ideas, and comments with me. The work you do makes such a difference to so many, and in so many ways. Thank you.

Dani Porter Born, teacher at Dodge Nature Preschool and photographer at http://daniporterborn.zenfolio.com: Once again your photos have made this whole thing worth looking at. And to Megan Gessler, director of Natural Beginnings Early Childhood Program, Kendall County Forest Preserve District, Illinois, thank you and your colleagues so much for your generosity.

I also give huge thanks to the children, families, teachers, and directors of early childhood programs I've been able to learn from over the years: the Dodge Nature Preschool in Saint Paul, Children's Country Day School in Mendota Heights, Tamarack Nature Center, and Prior Lake–Savage Area Schools in Minnesota. Thank you for sharing your everyday moments with me. Rachel, Jessica, Anna, and Annie—thank you for sharing photos, stories, and inspiring examples of this most meaningful work.

Thank you to David Sobel, for your support of this work, for continuing to be such an advocate for children in their natural habitat, and for teaching and inspiring so many grownups to do the same!

Much appreciation to the folks (and funders) who have set a place at the "big kids' table" for early childhood in recent years: National Science Teachers Association, National Council of Teachers of Mathematics, and many influential others, including the Natural Start Alliance and the North American Association for Environmental Education, and the Children & Nature Network.

Thanks to the educators at the Bakken Museum in Minneapolis, the Science Museum of Minnesota, Works Museum in Bloomington, Minnesota, and the Exploratorium in San Francisco for sharing graphics and answering my many questions about inquiry investigations, STEM, and learning. Also, thanks for making me feel like a kid again.

Thank you to the team at Redleaf for your editorial support, design work, moral support, deadlines, and commitment to this work.

And, finally, to Fred Rogers: I wish you were still here. We need you more than ever.

Introduction

WHAT IS IT THAT MAKES NATURE so appealing to young children? Children are drawn to the natural world for many reasons. They are intrigued by being in a place where there are animals' homes, a place that is not created by adults. Nature offers a limitless variety of sounds, smells, textures, and things to be curious about. Nature offers children a glimpse into a special world where they feel reverence and awe. Nature offers children the opportunity to explore, to move freely, and to test the limits of one's own body through climbing, jumping, and moving over uneven terrain. For the young child, this challenge is invigorating and empowering. In recent years, those who work with young children have recognized the value in providing children with nature-based opportunities to learn, play, relax, and just be. More and more programs, schools, and even home-based care settings embrace the natural world and strive to create opportunities for children to spend time outside, exploring and playing, as children do best.

Nature is appealing for many reasons.

The number of nature-based preschools has increased dramatically in recent years, and this growth shows no signs of slowing. I celebrate this evolution.

Hidden within children's adventures and investigations outdoors are countless moments when they are engaging in some of the fundamental practices associated with science, technology, engineering, and mathematics (STEM) learning. These are practices like asking questions, making predictions, creating solutions to problems through building and making things, seeking patterns, sorting and organizing materials, communicating their ideas, and more. I believe this is why nature is such a perfect context for teaching STEM: it's a context in which children feel more freedom, and in their unstructured play and investigation, their natural tendencies and thinking patterns emerge readily. Nature also offers limitless diversity in terms of sensory input and opportunities to investigate questions. It also offers a variety of textures, sounds, colors, shapes, and spaces in which to play. It's always changing, which means that children are constantly inspired to ask questions, explore, and learn through nature's many provocations.

Furthermore, with all the research that has come out in recent years (explored more deeply in chapter 2), we know that being in nature is good for children's health and well-being. It provides children with opportunities to exercise their bodies, their minds, and, yes, even their spirits. Nature offers a place for children to be challenged and tested, a place to explore and question, a place where they can be loud or quiet, solitary or among friends. For this reason, it's a great equalizer: children of all backgrounds, learning styles, and abilities can benefit from time outdoors.

Nature play and exploration are valuable and important experiences in their own right. Many of today's teachers are aware of the benefits to young children and are eager to implement more nature-based learning. It's clear to most educators that young children feel deep joy, freedom, curiosity, reverence, and awe in natural settings. My hope in writing this book is to help connect those feelings to science, technology, engineering, and math practices, because children engage in these practices when in nature play, often without realizing it. There are so many opportunities to capitalize on children's interest in science, technology, engineering, and math, as well as their curiosity and excitement about nature. And the ways that children engage in natural learning about STEM parallels the way they play outdoors: with curiosity, persistence, a spirit of inquiry, and a collaborative nature. Since nature is a source of positive feelings and a constant source of inspiration and questions for children, it's a perfect context in which to teach STEM. Teaching in nature can connect STEM learning to a sense of joy and wonder.

Nature can inspire feelings of joy and awe.

Nature offers a variety of textures, sounds, smells, and sights to capture the attention of every child. It can calm some children while stimulating others, making it a place for learning where all children can thrive. It also gives them opportunities to practice self-regulation by managing their behavior, voice, and movements to match their surroundings. The sheer variety of sensory input can have a positive effect on children's minds and bodies as they exercise their senses of sight, smell, hearing, and touch all at the same time.

This rich mix of benefits and attractions makes nature a perfect context in which to teach. The physical challenges presented by natural environments can help young children develop relationships with one another, play more creatively, and indulge their curiosity about the world. Within this context there is enough variation in material and environment, such as sticks, water, rocks, mud, animals, nests, weather, and more, to provide children with an infinite variety of opportunities to learn, grow, and understand the world.

I do not mean to suggest in this book that teachers make outdoor time more academically oriented. However, I do suggest that teachers recognize the innate tendency of young children to engage in the practices associated with STEM—observing, asking questions, investigating, and exploring—and to intentionally support those tendencies. I also believe that if intentionally connecting nature time to STEM teaching makes it easier, more appealing, or more likely that teachers or staff will support nature play, so much the better.

If, through allowing their classes more outdoor playtime, teachers begin to witness and develop an understanding of children's natural tendencies to "think STEM" and this in turn helps to justify more outdoor time, then I fully embrace these connections. We now know that getting children outdoors can engage them in STEM thinking skills and practices in a way that indoor experiences simply can't, so teachers should have access to all of the support and resources they need to encourage such efforts.

Children learn through play in natural settings.

Many teachers take children outdoors frequently—but only to structured playgrounds and only for recess. I agree that any time outside is time well spent, but that tendency perpetuates the common perspective that there is some difference between outdoor time and "learning time." This books offers countless reasons to take children outdoors for play *and* learning, since the two happen in tandem.

Many educators believe that children should be allowed to play freely in natural settings without any interference from teachers and without the added pressure of making it into an academic exercise. I believe that children need extended periods of playtime in natural settings and that playtime in itself is intrinsically valuable and important. I am an avid supporter of nature play and believe that, whenever possible, children's investigations and explorations in the natural world should be child directed, interest driven, and free of adult interference or direction. However, I also believe there is plenty of room to play with between these two positions—with early childhood STEM learning, the teacher's role is as more of a facilitator and supporter than director.

What's in This Book?

This book helps readers understand how to support children in developing, demonstrating, and articulating STEM-related thinking skills, including approaches to problem solving and collaboration, as well as other important "soft skills" that are good for children's development. It is also a resource for readers who want to nurture young children's love for the natural world and their innate tendencies toward exploration and investigation, building, and numbers, and it helps readers approach nature play with STEM learning in mind.

Teachers have many opportunities to make connections to the STEM disciplines by being intentional with exploration, materials, and purpose when they venture outdoors with their students. Even simple shifts such as listening to children's questions about nature, listening for children to use certain words, or taking certain actions can help you "tune in" to the natural STEM engagement that children experience in nature. And this book will help you identify ways to shift your questioning and your engagement with students to help them think more deeply about STEM as they play and enjoy nature.

This book also aims to help you recognize the numerous opportunities already available and to use them as "starts," or jumping-off points, to dive more deeply into a STEM topic, concept, or practice. I think of these frequent, ongoing moments as "STEM starts." In the world of gardening, "plant starts" are small seedlings that have been sown and are ready to be planted and take root, and these STEM starts that appear throughout the book are similar. They can serve as starting points for investigations that you and your students will engage in, and, like the roots of a plant, your shared engagement will grow deeper over time.

Positive experiences in the natural world can have a far-reaching impact on young children. You never know what may spark an interest in science, or what experience may shed light on a child's understanding of a mathematical concept. The goal of this book is to provide those who work with young children with practical suggestions, ideas, resources, and lessons for implementing science, technology, engineering, and math activities that are responsive to the developmental needs of young children. While not an activity book, it does contain suggestions for deepening your explorations outdoors and for looking differently at children's play. I have done my best to offer content, strategies, and practices that are developmentally appropriate. This work is informed by the recommendations and research backed by nationally recognized organizations such as the National Science Teachers Association, the National Council of Teachers of Mathematics, the National Academy of Engineering, the International Technology and Engineering Educators Association, the National Association for the Education of Young Children, and the North American Association for Environmental Education.

How Do I Use This Book?

Chapter 1, "What Is STEM?," provides a short overview of STEM and why it is so widely recognized and seems to be such a hot topic in education today. It explains why STEM disciplines are important in the early years and addresses their role in the achievement gap.

Chapter 2, "Why Kids Need Nature," contains some of the latest research on the role of nature in early childhood, including risks, benefits, and the relationship between nature and STEM learning. It offers examples of children's natural engagement in nature play and how their questions, investigations, and explorations can serve as perfect entry points into deeper STEM learning.

In chapter 3, "An Overview of the STEM Disciplines," you will find an explanation of the STEM disciplines, including the fundamental STEM thinking skills and practices common across disciplines. It offers teachers and parents a full understanding of those skills and practices and how they work together.

Chapter 4, "Building on a Strong STEM Foundation," gives more insight into additional approaches, such as inquiry-based learning, soft skills associated with STEM, tools for documentation, learning dispositions, and productive questioning techniques.

Many of the questions children raise outdoors provoke curiosity that lasts and lasts.

Chapter 5, "Putting It All Together," provides a road map for evaluating your own program and resources, and helps you think about how you might make subtle, or not so subtle, changes to your approaches and practices, and how you can begin to integrate STEM more deeply in your work.

Finally, in chapter 6, you will find STEM Starts that will help you think about specific activities or actions you can take to connect your work and your nature explorations to particular concepts within the domains of science, engineering, and math. Chapter 6 contains over 120 STEM starts to get your creative juices flowing.

The appendices contain other useful resources as well. Appendix A includes links to resources such as statements from nationally-recognized organizations that focus on the STEM disciplines and how they relate to early learners. I have also listed books, periodicals, and websites that I have found particularly valuable. In appendix B, you will find a list of specific practices associated with each of the STEM disciplines, along with a chart of examples of what they look like in children's nature play. This chart also includes recommendations for specific materials or investigations that will help provoke STEM engagement. Appendix C briefly addresses standards, recommendations, and guidelines for anyone wishing to incorporate more nature-based play and learning in their early childhood setting. Appendix D provides a chart for you to quickly connect STEM Starts to "crosscutting concepts," ideas that bind together the STEM disciplines.

When you are aware of the scientific, engineering, and mathematical practices that characterize STEM, and you are open to developmentally appropriate uses of technology to support learning, you can start to "think STEM" during outdoor excursions and use children's questions and ideas to start investigations or prompt questions.

While this book focuses more on the processes and practices of STEM than on the concepts and content within the disciplines, it is important to recognize that comfort and confidence with a particular subject area or discipline is crucial for teachers to be able to implement it effectively. Understanding the subject matter is critical. Identifying the basic concepts that are appropriate for early learners is the first step, and then it is the teacher's responsibility to learn and understand those concepts so that she may be intentional and thoughtful about deepening children's learning through meaningful inquiry. Resources are available to build your background knowledge about STEM content, several of which are listed in the resources in appendix A. Concern for pedagogy is central to all of that, and one goal of this book is to help you reflect on your own approaches to teaching.

In addition to questioning their own capabilities to teach STEM, many educators feel challenged by the need to link STEM teaching to an already packed curriculum. In early childhood settings, this is sometimes less the case than in upper grades, where teachers are pressured to fill every hour with material that will be "on the test" later. Throughout this book, I have tried to show how engaging outdoor experiences naturally lead students into STEM practices, which instructors can then enhance through intentional guidance.

Teachers can support children's investigations in many ways.

"Think STEM"

There are many ways to engage children in STEM practices that complement what you are already doing in the classroom. As an educator who works with young children, you likely have already spent a lot of time introducing concepts, topics, or ideas from scientific fields. For example, when playing with light and shadows, you are introducing concepts from the domain of physics. When your students play with mud and puddles in springtime, they are exploring properties of earth sciences, including earth materials, the water cycle, and more. Conversations about weather, seasonal changes, and temperature fluctuations are explorations into the field of meteorology. Block building is a young child's first foray into the field of structural engineering. Rhyming games, patterns, and movement activities connect to mathematics, though you may not realize this just yet. While you may not have recognized or articulated the STEM learning taking place, many of the typical day-to-day activities that occur in early childhood education settings already connect to STEM.

You can demonstrate your own enthusiasm for children's interests in STEM in many ways, as well as support their learning through what you say and how you present materials and opportunities, and even by your own attitude. You will not only help children become familiar with important content-specific concepts and principles, but more significantly, you will help instill a comfort and ease with the practices we associate with STEM that can have a long-lasting effect on a child's perspective and future success in school. Ideally, this book will help you find new freedom and joy in thinking about STEM and the practices associated with STEM thinking. When you do, the children in your classroom will certainly pick up on it, and it will impact their approaches to learning as well as their confidence and interest in STEM.

What Is STEM?

By now, *STEM* has become a household term. The acronym, which stands for "science, technology, engineering, and math," was first introduced in 1990 by the National Science Foundation to recognize the way that the disciplines of science, technology, engineering, and mathematics are interconnected in the workforce, and to emphasize that these subjects should not be taught in isolation because they rarely appear in isolation in the real world. The term is most commonly used within the context of education. Before we get into that discussion, though, it's helpful to clarify what each of the four STEM domains includes.

The domain of science includes life science, earth and space science, physical science, and other fields that are commonly drawn upon to build an understanding of the world. Countless mysteries lie before us that we are only beginning to understand, such as outer space, the mysteries of the oceans and water systems, and the immense biodiversity of the planet. Science helps us refine our existing understandings and provides us a context in which to build on our knowledge. It allows us to make new discoveries to better grasp our place in the universe. Science also helps us understand and think critically about some of the major problems that we confront today, such as climate change, decreasing water supplies, global food inequities, public health crises, and more.

Technology includes all of the human-made digital and nondigital tools that we

Nature-based play settings and materials offer a lot of different sensory input and physical challenges.

use to understand science, solve our problems, meet our needs and desires, and navigate our world, virtually and in reality. While many adults think specifically about electronic and digital tools when they hear the word *technology*, it actually refers to any tool that is used to fulfill a human need. Technology can be an electronic tablet, a remote-controlled car, a tennis shoe, even a piece of tape.

The field of engineering is where the disciplines of science, technology, and math come together; it is where problems are solved via the creation of solutions: objects, systems, or processes designed to meet human needs or make life better. Engineering fields include (but are not limited to) electrical engineering, mechanical engineering, chemical engineering, and civil engineering.

Mathematics is the language that weaves all of the domains together. At its heart, mathematics is about logic, order, and reasoning. Math allows us to make sense of the world and communicate our ideas. Math provides a language through which we can express relationships, patterns, systems, quantity, space, and shape.

Magnifiers and natural objects are commonly used in early childhood settings.

Integration Matters

Just as the STEM disciplines are linked together in real life, they need to be linked together in the classroom to be most potent. Teachers can address each subject in isolation, and children will build knowledge, just as they do with other subjects. But STEM is far more meaningful and the learning is far more engaging when the disciplines are integrated and intentionally connected. Integration of the disciplines helps students see and make real-life connections. This makes STEM much more relevant and meaningful to them. In chapter 5, I describe more specifically how and why it is so important to integrate the disciplines.

Indeed, throughout the field of education, there is a sincere recognition of the need for better, more closely linked and more intentional instruction of these disciplines. In recent years, there has been a steep increase in the number of schools and other educational settings that highlight STEM education. In some elementary schools, this takes the form of dedicated blocks of time when children learn STEM subjects, or it may be an approach that more intentionally integrates STEM across other disciplines. A growing number of schools are self-applying the title "STEM school" in an attempt to address the need for high-quality, integrated STEM education. What this integration looks like in practice varies quite a bit. It might range from one or two hours each week for STEM-specific content classes to a drop-in enrichment program, all the way to a fully integrated curriculum that connects all disciplines to STEM through intentional links of content, practice, and reflection.

Some early childhood education settings are following this lead by including more science and technology in their programs, but many educators and program directors lack the experience, confidence, or logistical support to fully attempt a more integrated approach to STEM education in the early childhood setting. By better understanding what characteristics and elements make up each of the disciplines, you may be pleased to learn that you already address STEM more than you thought. Knowing this may make the idea of integrating disciplines feel more approachable. If you want to become truly intentional about high-quality STEM education, you can use specific strategies and approaches to help children deepen their comfort and fluency within the STEM practices and dispositions (the attitudes associated with learning) that are so important for school and that will positively impact children for years to come.

When we hear about STEM on the news, in popular magazines, and in other media, it's usually that the United States is facing a "STEM shortage." This press coverage often laments the fact that fewer and fewer college students are choosing to major in and select careers associated with science, technology, engineering, or math despite the fact that skills in those areas are in high demand and necessary for a growing number of current and future jobs. There has been a well-defined need for teachers to support the development of children's learning in the STEM areas because of the perceived and documented lags our nation has faced in these areas. Although most young people don't think about their careers until middle or high school, ideally, they can develop positive feelings and attitudes at an early age that may impact their choices later on. Educators and others recognize that students' attitudes, self-efficacy, interest, and excitement about the STEM disciplines are shaped at a very young age. There are surely serious implications if our nation's young people are self-selecting out of STEM careers, but STEM education is not all about career choices and national security.

There is also an increased focus on STEM within the world of classroom education. New books, materials, and curricula that promise to improve STEM outcomes for learners are brought to market regularly. Many professional development opportunities and conferences offer teachers new and engaging ways to bring STEM into the classroom. Curriculum kits and exciting new gadgets and gizmos abound, each promising to enliven STEM and "hook" students. Schools and school districts scramble to seek funding for technology and materials to incorporate curricula and programs that will better prepare our young people for college and STEM careers.

Despite this somewhat recent increase in attention and the excitement surrounding STEM learning, STEM is far from a buzzword. For young children, the practices inherent in STEM are foundational to later success in school and are important for social-emotional development (Duncan et al. 2007). As they engage in STEM learning, young children gain an important set of habits of mind and practices that can significantly impact their future educational outcomes and academic success in any area.

The practices and processes associated with STEM subjects can also help strengthen children's cognitive health, intellectual growth, social-emotional development, and creative thinking. Educators try to determine the best ways to find links among the disciplines and to think about how to teach them in ways that make sense to young children and support their development.

But when teachers aren't comfortable or confident in their own knowledge or ability to effectively teach particular subjects, they tend to avoid them in the classroom or give them only perfunctory attention. Unlike middle and high school teachers who teach science and math classes, elementary and early childhood teachers are "generalists"—that is, they have to know a lot about a large variety of topics—so they naturally tend to concentrate on the subjects they feel most comfortable teaching. In other cases, teachers, ever more pressed for time, have to prioritize, and therefore spend a great deal of time on other subjects, like language arts, that appear on high-stakes, standardized tests, often to the exclusion of subjects such as science and engineering, which usually do not appear on standardized tests in the primary years.

STEM in the Early Years

In the early childhood and primary educational settings, when specific hours each day aren't allotted to specific subjects, less time is spent on the STEM subjects. This deficit can have a significant impact on children's learning. Children's attitudes around science and math are shaped in the early years, and by the time they are in elementary school, those attitudes can be very difficult to change (Archer et al. 2010). By as early as fourth grade, many children have decided that they are not interested in science. There are a number of reasons for this. The attitudes of the adults in a child's life toward these subjects can influence the child's attitude and interest. As with so much in the world of the young child, adults' messages and communication greatly affect children's attitudes, feelings, and self-efficacy with material.

Moreover, when teachers aren't comfortable or don't feel confident in teaching a subject, they tend to communicate that unease either directly or indirectly to their students. "I'm not a math person!" is a familiar lament of many early childhood educators. Teachers should be aware of the evidence that children pick up on adults' attitudes about, discomfort with, and lack of knowledge in STEM content areas and their lack of confidence in teaching these subjects. As a result, children may miss the opportunity to develop an interest in STEM or find their nascent curiosity stifled by a disinterested teacher who, unintentionally, doesn't nurture that child's interest and help take it to the next level.

When teachers are better equipped to teach STEM, they will be more likely to include it as part of their regular work in the classroom. They will also be more confident in their ability to recognize and support children's natural curiosity about STEM and the practices that engage them in STEM-related exploration. The result will be that children are more engaged, more curious about STEM content and practices, and therefore more likely to stay interested in the STEM disciplines as they continue through school. They may even go on to pursue STEM-related careers.

Children are inherently curious about everything they encounter, making the early years a perfect time for STEM investigations.

STEM beyond the Classroom

Beyond career choices, STEM literacy is important for all citizens. STEM literacy affords adults the capacity to critically examine issues, carefully evaluate data and research, and make thoughtful conclusions and interpretations. It is crucial for making informed decisions and applying reason and understanding to issues that we confront today, from social and consumer concerns to environmental, global, and even political issues.

This is not to suggest that young children should be presented with those tough issues that confront our society; there is plenty of time for that in the later grades, when children are emotionally and intellectually ready to wrestle with them. There is, however, great value in providing opportunities for children to construct knowledge in STEM practices and content areas so that they are better equipped to understand and think critically about those issues as they mature. Even in the early years, before children begin to grapple with societal issues, basic awareness of STEM concepts, practices, and principles will lay a foundation for building deeper understanding of those issues later on. When young children have little exposure to STEM, they will be less engaged in the subjects as they proceed through school and are likely to be less "STEM-literate" as adults.

Just as we know that in early childhood the foundation for skills such as reading and language arts is laid very early through positive, authentic experiences, so too are the foundations for habits of mind and practices associated with STEM. As noted earlier, the STEM disciplines are associated with a set of thinking skills and practices that benefit children's cognitive, social-emotional, and intellectual development. Nature-based STEM learning can also have a positive effect on children's physical and mental health. This can have far-reaching effects on a child's academic success.

STEM and the Achievement Gap

Can a young child's fluency with a subject in kindergarten predict her future success as a learner? There is a growing body of research that says yes. Children's general knowledge in kindergarten has been shown to be a strong predictor of their knowledge and achievement—even in other disciplines such as language arts—up through the eighth grade. High-quality STEM education is especially important for children from disadvantaged backgrounds, who on average demonstrate lower levels of competence with STEM prior to school entry, and once they enter school, these gaps persist or even widen (McCoach et al. 2006; Reardon 2011).

When children lack a foundation in STEM, it naturally follows that they will have difficulty in later grades with classroom material focused on the STEM disciplines. Evidence suggests this may lead to behavioral challenges, such as a lack of ability to persist at tasks and difficulty staying focused on tasks, which may also be ongoing factors in low achievement (Duncan et al. 2007). When children struggle to understand content knowledge and practices associated with their school subjects, the result can be feelings of frustration, failure, and low self-esteem, which can set children up for ongoing struggles throughout their academic years.

Nature-based STEM learning can have a positive effect on children's development and academic success.

It's particularly important to consider the effect of these factors with regard to children in underserved communities. There is a disproportionate rate of opportunity and achievement (often referred to as the "achievement gap") among racial-, ethnic-, and language-minority children as compared to their white peers (US Census Bureau 2012). These children's families often experience greater economic disadvantage as compared to their white counterparts. According to the National Assessment of Educational Progress (NAEP), children from low-income families tend to demonstrate low levels of math competence by the time they enter kindergarten, and as their schooling continues, if they do not receive support, these gaps continue to widen (McCoach et al. 2006; Reardon 2011). This is true for science as well: many children from low-income and minority populations not only lack content knowledge but have fewer opportunities for high-quality science education. Schools that have fewer financial resources often offer fewer academic opportunities for children and have a harder time retaining the best-qualified teachers. They may have fewer material resources, such as tools and technology to aid in children's investigations. They may have limited or no access to natural areas in which to teach outdoors. There may be a shortage of involved parents to support teachers. Add to that the lack of teachers who understand how to teach STEM in a developmentally appropriate way, and it's clear this is an issue that demands urgent attention, and we must address it.

Further compounding these barriers, the high cost of quality early care and education programs makes them unaffordable for many families, placing high-quality early education opportunities out of reach. In many regions, state-subsidized early care and education settings are the only option for many families, and the quality of care among these settings varies widely. The educational credentials and qualifications of providers vary as well. School district or corporate child care programs often require employees to hold a four-year degree and, in some cases, a teaching license; however, this is not the case in a vast number of settings, particularly those serving low socioeconomic status communities. Since early childhood education is among the lowest-paying careers, many adults who work in this field have little incentive and often lack the financial means to pursue coursework or professional development beyond the minimum required by their programs. Given the challenge that many educators face with teaching STEM, and the fact that struggling districts or programs often can't afford to pay educators much more than minimum wage, it isn't surprising that STEM education is an afterthought in many early care settings.

Understanding the benefits of high-quality STEM education is central to addressing these challenges. It's particularly urgent that teachers commit to providing high-quality experiences with STEM for *all* learners in order to close the achievement gap, simply because it's the right thing to do.

ALL CHILDREN DESERVE HIGH-QUALITY STEM EDUCATION

Using nature as a context for STEM learning can have positive, far-reaching implications. Children living in disadvantaged circumstances are likely to have increased anxiety and experience continuous high levels of stress as a result of trauma, high mobility, food insecurity, and other conditions. The positive effects of time spent in nature on well-being—such as reduced anxiety, improved peer-to-peer relationships, and self-confidence—can help children struggling with these issues as well. While educators are beginning to realize that access to nature is a social justice issue, so too is access to a high-quality STEM education.

All young children have a natural tendency to explore, to ask questions, to investigate, to create and test things out, and to seek patterns and order in the world. These are characteristics associated with the practices and habits of mind inherent in STEM learning. Increased time spent in natural settings also leads to more-cohesive classrooms and stronger social-emotional development, and offers additional benefits to children's mental health. An increasing number of early care and education providers want to take children outdoors more often and see real value in nature-based learning. There are many ways to partake in the benefits of nature-based learning and play.

Why Kids Need Nature 2

IN RECENT YEARS, EDUCATORS HAVE BECOME more aware of the importance of taking children outdoors for play, learning, and even rest time. Books like *Last Child in the Woods* by Richard Louv have spurred new interest among educators and parents in the role of nature in young children's lives. Many adults can recall childhood memories filled with experiences in the outdoors, from building forts and playing in secret worlds to climbing trees, swinging from branches, swimming in cool lakes, and hiking and camping with family. These memories are some of the most powerful and potent for many of us, and that has led to a sense of alarm as we have watched today's children become increasingly separated from nature. Whether the result of a lack of resources, competing demands for children's attention, or shifting parental attitudes toward time in the outdoors, the evidence is clear: children these days are spending less time outdoors than children from generations past. There are significant implications for how this may affect children's growing sense of connection to the outdoors, their sense of stewardship, relationships with animals, and even relationships with other children. It also has implications for their own social-emotional development, physical and mental health, and ability to manage stress.

The good news is that more and more educators and parents are becoming aware of the value of nature and are searching for increased opportunities to get children outdoors. There has been an increase in resources for teachers looking to link

Climbing trees can become a cherished childhood memory.

nature to the curriculum; an increase in workshops, conferences, and other professional development opportunities; and there are even nature-based preschool conferences and associations that support educators in this important work. At the time of this writing, there are more than 150 nature-based preschools and kindergartens. The Natural Start Alliance (www.naturalstart.org), a coalition that promotes connecting children with nature, defines nature-based preschools as early childhood settings that "put nature at the heart of the curriculum and use nature to support children's development and environmental education." Momentum is building.

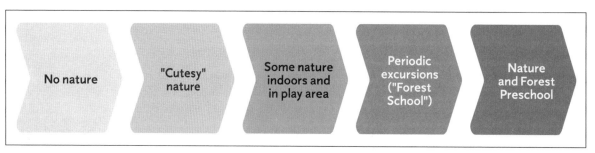

This growing public understanding of the value of nature in young children's lives has led to an increased appreciation of environmental education, also called "nature-based learning" for young children. The North American Association for Environmental Education defines early childhood environmental education as "a holistic concept that encompasses knowledge of the natural world as well as emotions, dispositions, and skills." Referring to educator and outdoor play advocate Ruth Wilson's list of some of those emotions and dispositions, the association describes them as "a sense of wonder, appreciation for the beauty and mystery of the natural world . . . the development of problem-solving skills and the development of interest in and appreciation for the world around us" (North American Association for Environmental Education 2010, 2).

Educators are increasingly interested in capitalizing on young children's inherent interest in the natural world to enhance learning. Indeed, there is a growing body of research that supports the use of nature as a setting in which to learn, and some studies suggest that students learn more through outdoor experiences than in traditional classroom settings (Cronin-Jones 2000).

A sense of wonder for the beauty and mystery of the natural world develops in early childhood.

Those who work with young children are clearly aware of nature's many benefits to children's mental and physical health and its positive impact on classroom dynamics, and they realize the positive intellectual impact that learning outdoors can have. What they may not yet understand, however, is the uniquely rich opportunity that nature presents for teaching the disciplines of science, technology, engineering, and math.

The Role of Nature in Learning

There are a variety of educational benefits to being in nature, including enhancing soft skills or dispositions toward learning, as well as offering a myriad of academic and intellectual benefits. Natural settings support prosocial behavior, in other words, behaving in ways that help others without the expectation of external rewards (Mussen and Eisenberg 1978). Early childhood educators might also refer to this characteristic as empathy or generosity. Children tend to act in ways that are kind and supportive of one another in natural settings, and there are a number of factors that may explain why.

Perhaps nature is a particularly rich setting for children to engage in these positive prosocial behaviors because it offers so many opportunities to engage with other life-forms. In my book *Connecting Children and Animals in Early Childhood*, I discuss how young children view animals as inherently valuable, important, and interesting simply because "they are." Children are attuned to animals' intrinsic worth. In natural settings this feeling is demonstrated through caring for garden creatures, asking questions, or otherwise demonstrating curiosity about the behavior or life cycle of common animals such as insects, birds, and squirrels, and wondering about the world these creatures inhabit. When children concern themselves with animals through anticipating their needs (such as for food, water, or shelter), they are demonstrating the quality of caring. This is important because it helps children develop a sense of responsibility toward other living creatures as well as their own sense of power and autonomy.

Children have a deep, innate love for all kinds of animals.

In addition to supporting prosocial development, nature offers children plenty of opportunities to practice perspective taking (which leads to empathy) when children are engaged in dramatic play. Pretending to be animals is a clear example of perspective taking. In doing so, children imagine the experience of another living creature. Watch young children when they are playing at being animals and you will likely observe many ways that children understand animals: how they move, how they interact with one another, the sounds they make, and more. They "try on" the life of that animal, even if just for a short time, and this helps them not only to construct knowledge and understanding of animals but to feel empathy and consideration for other creatures.

Play in natural settings also often leads to collaborative building projects (such as creating houses or fairy gardens together) in which children are motivated to work together and cooperate, anticipating one another's needs and sharing resources. Even children who prefer to play alone can create small worlds out of treasures found on the forest floor, making homes for imaginary creatures demonstrating an innate sense of altruism and generosity.

In addition to showing their concern and curiosity toward creatures both real and imagined, children also wonder about plants and have real questions about what plants experience. If one child peels bark off of a tree, there is likely at least one other child in the class who will exclaim, "Stop it! You're hurting the tree!" Children either inherently know or have learned that trees are living things, and in crying out in the tree's defense, they are attempting to sort out their understanding about what it means for a tree to be a living thing.

STEM Start

If you hear children express the sentiment that the plant or tree is "dead" (and you're sure it isn't), instead of verbally correcting their misconception, try engaging them in investigation. Invite them to come up with a list of characteristics of living plants. How do they know when a plant or tree is alive? (Some suggestions: they grow, they sprout leaves, the leaves are green, they may display flowers.) Create your list together and then develop a plan for how you can observe the tree over time to see if it exhibits any characteristics as the seasons change. This engages children in reflecting on what they know and referring to their prior knowledge about plants and trees (identifying characteristics they have seen in living trees) and in predicting what might happen to the tree you're studying over time. They will also practice observing as the tree changes in response to the temperature and amount of sunlight. You may also engage them in developing tools for measuring the plant or tree (such as a tape measure, counting links, rope, or other ways). It will be hard to see significant changes in tree growth, but herbaceous plants (plants without woody stems) will grow quickly over a growing season, and their height can be measured as change observed over time.

Consider a remark made during one class's outdoor excursion to a shrubby forest edge near the school yard. Ruby asks, "Do birds get cold in winter? Maybe we should put out some cotton balls for their nests."

In this example, Ruby demonstrates social-emotional awareness as well as scientific knowledge about birds. A question such as this indicates an understanding not only that birds are living things with feelings and physical vulnerabilities (getting cold) but also a grasp of how birds are the same as or different than she is (because she herself has been cold). Finally, the idea to provide cotton for their nests indicates a desire to care for the birds and to demonstrate that caring through providing

Children are naturally curious about trees, no matter the season.

something that would help meet the bird's basic needs. She is also drawing on her knowledge of birds and bird behavior to develop an idea about how to help them by making a nest for shelter.

This rich statement made by the child demonstrates perspective taking. Phyllis Kahn, a researcher on young children and nature, speculated that when young children develop empathy toward animals and show that empathy through prosocial behaviors (such as wanting to feed the birds or provide nesting material for them) that empathy is generalized to include other people as well (Kahn 1997).

One reason that STEM and nature-based education complement each other so well is that many of the dispositions and skills described above are also those associated with the disciplines of science, engineering, and math. (I refer to technology in early childhood as a set of tools with which children can develop knowledge and skills.)

The fundamental process skills and habits of mind that early childhood STEM learning supports go hand in hand with the ideas and outcomes of nature-based learning and natural settings in early childhood. These ideas underscore the importance of joy and other positive emotions as having a central role in education. In early childhood, learning is so much more than a cognitive process. In early childhood nature-based STEM, it's crucial that children feel joy, pleasure, and wonder as they play, learn, and explore. Those are the feelings that will keep them coming back for more.

Children want to care for animals and are curious about what they need.

Large wide open spaces offer children plenty of room to run and cavort.

Incorporating early experiences with STEM should help children construct knowledge, but more importantly, it should help children achieve fluency with the practices of STEM and the dispositions that develop through engagement with those practices. This can have far-reaching implications.

Research has consistently found additional benefits to unstructured play in natural settings. Children's play is often consistently longer in duration, more complex, and more likely to consist of mixed age groups. The stimulation provided by nature—loose parts, hiding places, interesting sounds, smells, and textures, uneven terrain and climbing surfaces to challenge little bodies—often results in deep play. Many teachers note that behavior challenges are minimized, perhaps because nature offers so many options and generally more space for children at play. Finally, nature lends itself to a variety of ways of playing, which means that children who want to engage in quiet solitary play have a place to do so, while those who seek out rough-and-tumble play have a place to do so too.

Nature experiences also lend themselves to vocabulary development and communication skills. Children are curious to learn the names of plants, animals, and places, and they build their own vocabulary by learning new words as they need to. Nature gives children a reason to use those new words in context, which makes a big difference in language arts development. The word *pinecone* means a great deal more to a child who has a real pinecone to feel, hold, and smell than it does to the child who has only seen a picture of a pinecone. In the forest, during play, a child has an authentic reason to know the name of this object that looks and feels so unusual.

The benefits on attention and concentration, the positive impacts on children's relationship building, and the fact that children are innately attracted to natural settings means that nature also provides a unique and important context within which to engage children in STEM practices. The rich diversity of settings and materials naturally gives rise to observation and questions, which are important components of the process of inquiry and discovery.

With intentional engagement in the practices of STEM, detailed in chapter 3, you can help support children in developing these social-emotional skills. You can also start to recognize that through their explorations in nature, children are developing critical thinking skills, questioning, and abstract reasoning, as well as learning to confront and express their own ideas and fears appropriately, often within the context of exploration or play.

The Benefits of Outdoor Time and Recess

Playtime is an essential part of all early childhood programs and of raising children in general. It is central to both physical and social-emotional development. Play gives children opportunities to be loud and boisterous, which is generally not allowed indoors. And, as most educators know, young children need time and space to "burn off their energy" and "get the wiggles out." Play offers children ways to challenge themselves physically and to explore the dynamics of peer relationships, and it's the context in which most young children learn best. Many pre-K settings are play based, with a stronger focus on play than academics, whether indoors or out. Most early childhood advocates strongly support play in all its possible contexts, and I do too. There are many great places and ways to play, most of which have a direct positive impact on children. In this chapter, however, I'm referring specifically to the kind of play that happens during unstructured outdoor play, such as recess or field days, or unstructured time in nature. Be aware that the type, quality, and depth of play that occurs in nature-based settings is different than that which occurs on play structures or park equipment. While any outdoor time is preferable to time spent indoors, a setting other than a structured play yard with plastic equipment will do more to support children's development in many ways.

Nature offers opportunities for children to practice critical thinking and confront hesitation or fear.

While regulations vary from state to state and program to program, most people who work with young children are well aware of the benefits of unstructured outdoor play and are committed to making time for it each day. Many states require at least some daily physical activity for young children, though there are no federal requirements for outdoor time or recess. However, to combat a rapid rise in obesity rates among children ages six to eleven, the Centers for Disease Control and Prevention recommends at least one hour per day of physical activity for all children in grades K–6.

Also, an American Academy of Pediatrics' Council on School Health (2013) report cited a common problem of elementary schools reducing or eliminating recess time in order to ensure enough time for academic work. This is a false choice, especially as it relates to young children, since children actually engage in rich intellectual work and a significant amount of STEM learning during unstructured play, particularly when that time is spent in nature-based settings. Eliminating the opportunity for play is simply counterintuitive, since we know it is so important for children's health and well-being.

How Nature Supports the Development of Soft Skills

In addition to building vocabulary, social-emotional skills, and others, engaging in STEM outdoors can help nurture creativity, collaboration, critical thinking, and communication skills, a set of characteristics that are often referred to as "soft skills" or "twenty-first-century skills"—although most people would agree these are timeless qualities! Spending time outdoors in natural settings has a number of powerful effects on children, including increased self-control and better motor coordination, judgment, self-esteem, concentration, and ability to focus. In addition, children participate in more creative and cooperative play with others, and develop communication and critical thinking skills when given plenty of access to nature (Chawla 2012). These are the same inter- and intrapersonal skills that are facilitated through high-quality engagement in the practices of STEM.

Children have plenty of opportunities for creative play and social connections outdoors.

SELF-REGULATION

Self-regulation is defined as the ability to control one's body and emotions as well as managing one's focus and attention (Phillips and Shonkoff 2000). During nature play, children have many opportunities to practice self-regulation. Consider this example of children picnicking at the water's edge: A flock of ducks comes waddling up, hungry for scraps of torn sandwich crusts. Although children may squeal with delight and squirm with excitement, they discover that keeping relatively still and speaking in hushed tones will keep the ducks from flying away. They quickly realize what sorts of behavior—slow movements, quiet voices—will encourage the ducks to remain close, allowing the children more of a connection with the animals.

Other opportunities for self-regulation arise when children see insects and resist the urge to stamp or crush them, when the children hold still instead of frantically swatting at hovering bees during a picnic, or when they practice gentleness and care while holding a caterpillar. You can see children regulating their own bodies and managing their own strength and force even when they gently touch flowers or leaves without pulling or tearing them. In such instances, the children immediately learn that if they manage their actions, they get a desirable result, an immediate benefit such as more time with the animal, or an up close look at a beautiful flower. While there will likely always be a few children in any class who have difficulty self-regulating, nature offers plenty of opportunities and motivation to practice those skills.

Interactions with animals are perfect opportunities to practice self-regulation—keeping still is hard!

PHYSICAL CAPACITY, RISK TAKING, AND CONFIDENCE

While all early childhood settings, whether indoors or out, intentionally include time for large-motor activity, nature presents unique physical challenges and risks that are very important to children's developing sense of balance and physical strength. These challenges are also important in children's overall awareness of safety, risk, and capacity. Nature presents many opportunities for children—even babies and toddlers—to move up, down, around, in, over, under, and through. They have freedom to move quickly or slowly and are challenged by the variety of textures, materials, and surfaces available to play on. As children learn to move their bodies through space, they need opportunities to expand and refine their physical skills. Physical challenges also support children's math learning as they engage in immersive experiences of spatial learning. More on that in chapter 3.

Nature play also affects children's understanding of their own physical abilities, strengths, and weaknesses. In nature

The risks and challenges presented by natural settings are important childhood experiences.

children take physical and cognitive risks both together and with others. They continuously test the limits of their own skills, understanding, and abilities through construction, manipulation of materials, and physical challenges such as climbing, jumping, or lifting. Taking initiative, identifying and taking appropriate risks, failing, succeeding, and conquering fears can all be particularly potent childhood experiences when they occur outdoors (Finch 2012).

Physical risk can be a challenging issue for any educator responsible for young children. Yes, there is always a risk of a scraped knee, a bumped head, even a fall from a tree. But the risk of extreme danger during nature play can be minimized by thoughtful educators who are able to manage for risk by allowing children to take "calculated risks"—risks that the children themselves can assess and confront when they feel ready. We must allow children a certain degree of freedom and risk in order for them to know what they are capable of. That way, when risks present themselves later in life, children are more confident and sure of their own ability to assess and manage risk. Each program has its own guidelines, regulations, and rules around risk, and different teachers have different levels of comfort with risk as well. An awareness of your own comfort level, as well as an understanding of the value of risk in children's nature play will help you make more intentional choices about risk in your program.

Children practice assessing and evaluating risks when engaged in nature exploration.

Nature play is a powerful catalyst for growth that helps children develop good judgment, persistence, courage, resiliency, and self-confidence. "Can I make it across the stream on that log?" "Should I climb one branch higher than I did yesterday?" "Can I jump from that boulder to the next one?" All of these questions require a certain intuitive understanding of spatial awareness, a sense of weight, balance, stability, and distance. The opportunity to think in this way comes naturally to young children and grows stronger when they are given the freedom to explore.

Finally, as children develop confidence and self-efficacy through confronting and overcoming physical challenges, they develop a sense of security and safety in the world. They learn to trust their bodies and assess what they are capable of. I believe it's important for children to know that they are confident, safe, and capable of handling a certain amount of risk as they grow and their "home range" expands to include larger areas, such as local parks and wild spaces.

CREATIVE PLAY

Nature provides children with limitless stimulation and opportunities for creative play. Since nature is so varied, it presents a richness of textures, temperatures, movements, colors, sounds, sights, and characters. Children have endless opportunities for open-ended play: they can use loose parts to manipulate their environment by changing it and constructing things such as forts or small worlds for play, and they can explore through collecting, sorting, lifting, organizing, and digging. The world of nature is a place where children can be driven by their imagination.

Children develop confidence as they confront and overcome the physical challenges that nature play presents.

DISCOURSE

One way that children construct knowledge together is through discourse, the act of discussing ideas and experiences with one another. Discourse helps them clarify their own thinking, articulate their understanding, and communicate about their experience and prior knowledge. In a community of learners such as a preschool classroom, knowledge is built together through shared conversation and the natural back-and-forth that is found in social interactions. Listening to children's discourse about their experiences and ideas can help you, the teacher, better understand what children are thinking about the phenomena they have just experienced. When you know where children are at in their thinking, you can help to fill in the gaps in their understanding by providing experience, asking the children productive questions, and helping them build on one another's ideas.

Consider this example: a group of first graders ventures to their outdoor school yard in late autumn. The school yard has one area filled with bird feeders and shallow dishes that provide water. The first graders have been using this area to watch and learn about birds since the beginning of the school year and are now considering different things they can do to help the birds prepare for winter.

"We need to make sure they have food," says Rosa.

"No, they're migrating south," says Oscar. "They're leaving town."

"They aren't going south; they are staying here all winter. They still need food and water," reports Miles.

"They need to make a nest so they can stay warm," says Deonte.

"They only need a nest for having babies," argues Oscar.

"How are they going to stay warm?" demands Deonte.

"They need shelter to stay warm, a house to go into," says Oscar.

"Well," says Grace, "we have our bird feeders and our watering hole (the class's name for the area where the set of shallow dishes is located), but they need some kind of place to find shelter 'cause winter is coming."

A lively discussion ensues about what the students could do for the birds. Some of the ideas they propose to one another include increasing the amount and type of food provided, assembling and erecting wooden birdhouses, installing an outdoor fire pit to generate heat, making other structures for the birds, and planting additional trees. The teacher listens carefully to the children's ideas and facilitates the conversation so that her students have a chance to respond to one another, and so that those who want to share their ideas can do so. This kind of conversation is typical for this group of students who have been using the outdoors for exploration since the beginning of the year. They demonstrate some prior knowledge about the needs of wild birds, including food, access to water, and shelter. They demonstrate knowledge that some species of birds will remain all winter long and others will migrate. They consider the resources that are available to the birds and discuss whether they need to change or improve the existing resources. In addition to showing evidence of a shared basic understanding of several scientific concepts, including bird behavior and basic needs, migration and seasonal changes, the children are engaging in a powerful practice of science: discourse. Not only does discourse help them to clarify their own thinking and understanding, but it allows them to generate new learning based on the knowledge and ideas put forth by their peers. Finally, in this example, discourse is one strategy that these children use for collaborative problem solving. They are using critical thinking skills to generate ideas based on what they know about birds and their needs, as well as how they might use the resources available to them.

CONCENTRATION AND FOCUS

Attention restoration theory holds that after extended time in natural settings where multisensory input abounds, individuals are better able to concentrate indoors (Kahn and Kellert 2002). According to this theory, when we are outdoors, there are so many things to attend to that it's difficult for our brains to attend to just one thing at a time, so awash are we in sensory information. Our brains enter a relaxed state of alertness. Once we return indoors, our attention has sharpened and we are better able to focus. Many educators who take children outdoors on a regular basis report that children seem more alert and better able to focus on "indoor tasks" after some time outside. In fact, some researchers are finding interesting correlations between the impact of time outdoors on children's attention and alertness, which has especially important implications for children with attention or sensory disorders (Kuo and Taylor 2004). More time spent in green space seems to have a positive effect on children's ability to pay attention and focus on tasks throughout the day. Some teachers like to begin their day with twenty minutes or so of free play outdoors, knowing that it will help children focus and attend to tasks more successfully upon returning indoors.

Natural settings can calm children and create a state of relaxed alertness, leading to better concentration indoors.

Structured Play vs. Nature-Based Settings

While the benefits of recess are well known, many educators are surprised to learn that there are significant differences between the advantages offered by outdoor play on structured playgrounds and those inherent to open-ended, unstructured nature-based play. Most early care and education settings have outdoor play structures and carefully manicured play yards, and that is where outdoor play happens. These centers have colorful plastic or metal post-and-platform play structures, which can certainly be fun for kids, but they don't offer children the variety of opportunities that a natural play setting provides.

Structured playgrounds offer little variety or challenge once children have mastered them.

Play structures, by their very nature, are compelling due to their bright colors and invitations for physical challenge. However, upon closer inspection, many of the commercial versions offer few ways for children to vary their physical movement. The choices offered by "traditional" play structures generally are to go up (the ladder or play wall), go down (the slide), go across (the bridge), and swing. Most of these actions are solitary in nature (unless a child asks to be pushed on the swing) and thus provide children with few opportunities for collaborative play or shared experience, which are so important for young children.

Many children quickly become bored by the limited opportunities that traditional play equipment presents. Once they go up the ladder and down the slide repeatedly, the typical play structure doesn't have much to offer. Children love to challenge their bodies; indeed, they seek out opportunities to test their capabilities, and once they have mastered the play equipment, they look for more difficult challenges. That is when they do things like climb up the slide, twist the swings, jump off platforms that are high enough to make teachers cringe, and more. They get tired of waiting for their turn to go down the slide, and arguments ensue. Furthermore, many educators who work with young children have mixed feelings about what behavior is allowed on play structures; for example, one teacher may feel it's okay to let children climb up the slide, while another teacher from the same program may forbid this behavior.

Children will enjoy playing on a simple hillside if given the opportunity.

On the other hand, when play structures are complemented by natural elements, such as proximity to trees, shrubs, or grassy areas, or when they are near edges of "wild places" (such as wooded areas or even landscaped areas), they present children with many more opportunities for creative physical play.

Nature-based play is play that occurs away from the play structure, soccer field, cement parking lot, or other highly controlled or managed environment. Natural areas can include forests, wetlands, and wetland edges, grassy fields or meadows, streams and creeks, and other settings with few human-made objects. A nature-based setting for play might include natural materials such as plants, stones, mud, sand, fallen logs, sticks, vines, flowers, and water. It could be as simple as a set of container gardens for exploration or could be a landscaped area where children are allowed to play. Many intentionally designed places for early

Some children enjoy the sensory pleasure of going barefoot in the mud.

childhood nature play include a rich diversity of plants to stimulate different senses, winding pathways to inspire a sense of adventure, child-sized hiding places, such as forts or willow huts, and terrain such as small hills for children to roll down. When given the choice, many young children seem to prefer playing in nature-based settings over manufactured or manicured ones (Zamani 2013).

Children use tools such as scoops for investigating the natural world.

The rich, multisensory context of nature allows children to take in information with all of their senses, and that information is ever changing. Think of dappled sunlight filtering through leaves, the subtle change in temperature when the clouds part and the warm sunshine touches your skin. The smell of muddy, wet ground warming in the springtime. The scent of a forest floor covered in pine needles, warming on a summer day. This type of sensory input helps to fully immerse children in their surroundings, providing them a rich experience. Variation in sensory input is deeply stimulating and interesting. It invites children to touch and explore, building knowledge and inspiring questions. It stimulates creative play through invoking a sense of wonder and delight.

Loose Parts as Elements for STEM Learning

Nature is full of loose parts, such as sticks, pinecones, shells, stones, and other open-ended objects. Parents and teachers can collect loose parts for free, and many people believe that loose parts from nature not only support children's play and development, but can also help foster connections with the natural world.

Toys designed with one specific purpose and one particular role are usually used by children in only one way. Hand children a basket of toy cars, and they will likely use the cars as, well, cars. The trains will always be trains. Action figures and dolls will consistently exhibit human behavior and do humanlike things.

Bring children out into nature, though, and watch how they integrate natural loose parts into their play. Pinecones, stones, sticks—all are wonderful, rich playthings full of possibility. Pinecones will be enlisted as characters in dramatic stories, food during pretend picnics, birds that can fly through the air, spaceships hurtling through space. They will be porcupines, hiding places for fairies, even hairbrushes. Rocks will be currency, cars, boats, or building materials. Flowers become jewelry.

Loose parts are materials that can be used for any purpose a child imagines.

What makes loose parts so good for STEM learning? Open-ended toys help foster creativity, collaboration, and sensory awareness. They offer countless opportunities for cognitive growth. Children who use open-ended toys intuitively know that these objects have multiple uses. In this way, open-ended play objects encourage divergent thinking and creativity.

Loose-part play also allows for rich cognitive skill development and mastery. It is full of variation, requiring mental flexibility and adaptability. Loose parts allow children opportunities to discover and master their environment by naming things and then assigning them roles, a skill that education pioneer Jean Piaget recognized as one of the most important building blocks of learning. If you are uneasy with the idea of children playing with sticks and stones (and if you are, don't worry, you are not alone!), you can work with the children to set some simple rules to keep everyone safe—for example, no sticks longer than your arm, no touching other people with sticks, or no hitting anything with sticks. I encourage you to allow these important elements to be a part of children's play.

Science and math skills are practiced through building and construction. Watch how children use small rocks as currency or practice their one-to-one correspondence as they pass them out to their friends. They may have heated debates as they consider whether or not everyone has the "same number" of rocks. Finally, they count together or weigh the rocks in their hands to test their theories. Loose parts challenge young minds to find new ways to organize, classify, sort, and arrange. See how children use loose parts such as rocks for measurement, to experiment with balance and weight, and to make observations about subtle details such as color and texture. Loose parts are also often used as elements of patterns and designs and for tangible explorations of symmetry, scale, and size, thereby engaging children in mathematical thinking.

Flowers can be used in dramatic play.

Children's imagination and language acquisition are strengthened through the narration, storytelling, and description that happen during dramatic play with loose parts. Listen to the children's words as they describe their objects and how they are used. They notice attributes like hardness and texture and they describe them. Children notice and pay attention to the variations and details present in loose parts, and this offers creative stimulation as well: just sit with a child and look together at a handful of stones. You may be surprised at what you learn!

Sticks challenge children to explore and make sense of the properties of texture, weight, and balance. If they use the sticks for fort building or structures, they are challenged to understand the dynamics of building, including balance, stacking, length, height, and geometry (spatial awareness) and may select their sticks or other building materials based on what they intend to build. Sticks can help children gain awareness and construct knowledge of tree species, seasons, life cycles, systems, and structures. No two sticks are alike in size, shape, color, heft, or function, providing children a lot of opportunity to sort, order, compare, and contrast materials.

Some children may at first be stymied by the idea of playing with sticks and rocks. Chances are these children have become accustomed to electronic toys or action figures and may simply have had few opportunities to play with simple objects from nature. Once they have had more time to play in natural settings, they will become more comfortable using natural materials and letting their imagination drive their play and investigation of found objects. The gift of free, unstructured time in nature will offer them plenty of opportunities to practice tuning in to their innate creativity, rich imagination, and playful engagement with natural materials.

These children have collected rocks and organized them by color.

This boy uses different-shaped blocks of ice as building blocks while also learning about the properties of water and temperature.

An Overview of the STEM Disciplines

ONE OF THE MOST EXCITING THINGS about teaching STEM in early childhood settings is that young children are naturally engaged in STEM most of the time. In this chapter, I examine each of the four disciplines of science, technology, engineering, and math and illustrate what each discipline typically looks like in the early childhood setting. I share examples of the thinking practices most commonly associated with each domain and provide suggestions for how you can increase children's level of engagement, particularly outdoors. Once teachers know what that engagement looks like, they are often pleased to see how many opportunities young children have throughout the day to "think STEM."

The STEM disciplines are so closely intertwined, and a review of recommendations provided in the resource section reveals plenty of overlap in the thinking skills and practices that learners demonstrate in each discipline. While the content of each discipline is quite exclusive, the processes and practices associated with *doing* each discipline are similar. Specific practices are associated with each discipline, but in many cases the practices overlap and complement one another. This chapter presents specific thinking practices and competencies identified by many organizations that focus on education in the STEM disciplines. They can serve as benchmarks or targets that you can look for as you observe children at play.

A girl inspects the underside of a milkweed leaf in search of caterpillars.

Science

Even if you don't have a deep understanding of basic science concepts, and even if your school doesn't have a science specialist or many science resources, science can be found everywhere. You are probably already doing a lot more science than you might think. This section will help you recognize the numerous opportunities and rich material all around you that can provide jumping-off points for meaningful investigations to support children's learning in science as well as in other subject areas.

Science investigations in early childhood can make a big difference in a child's life. Young children are filled with questions and love to explore and investigate their world. Science is a perfect context in which to do this, since the practices associated with the discipline are so closely aligned to children's natural ways of thinking, doing, and learning. Science education in early childhood can help children build an understanding of their world; it also helps them develop higher-order thinking skills, reasoning skills, and self-regulation. It can help children build vocabulary and create context in their world. Finally, engagement in science investigations can have far-reaching intellectual and social-emotional benefits.

THE DOMAINS OF SCIENCE

The term *science* actually refers to an enormous and very diverse field of study that is broadly organized into three major domains: earth and space science, life science, and physical science. Each of those domains includes numerous additional fields of specialization. For example, within the domain of life science, a zoologist is someone who studies animals. If she studies birds, she is also an ornithologist. She might study parasites that live on birds, making her a parasitologist as well.

Investigations of rocks are common in earth science.

Earth and space science refers to the study of the earth and its properties and atmosphere. Geography (the study of physical features of the earth), meteorology (the study of weather and climate), and geology (the study of rocks and minerals) are all branches of the broader domain of earth science. Generally speaking, any area of study that concentrates on features and natural history of the earth would fall into this category. In early childhood classrooms, earth science materials usually include rock and mineral sets, weather tools, such as rain gauges, and activities involving buoyancy, such as "sink or float." Air and wind, day and night, sand and soil, and seasons are other common themes that touch on earth science. Space science in the early childhood setting generally includes activities or units that focus on stars and planets, the night sky, and even the solar system.

Physical science refers to the study of the physical properties of the earth and its atmosphere, and nonliving things and inanimate objects around us. Physics, chemistry, and astronomy all fall into this category. Early childhood educators might include in their classrooms objects such as ramps, magnets, gears, and simple machines, as well as investigations or activities about light and shadows, colors, and fluids and solids.

Life science is the study of living things, such as plants and animals, and their relationships to one another. Biology, botany, ecology, and zoology are all domains within life science. Plants, animals, classroom pets, the human body, gardens, rain forests, oceans, and insects are all common topics for life science investigations in the early childhood setting.

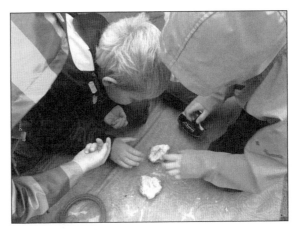

These children use magnifiers for a close-up look at geodes.

SCIENCE IN THE EARLY CHILDHOOD CLASSROOM

Many early care and education classrooms have a "science station" or nature table with intriguing objects and materials. These might be items found on nature hikes, seasonal items, gears, mirrors, magnets, or other objects, which often correspond to a theme, favorite story, or recent event that the class has experienced. The intent of a science station is usually to deepen students' interest and exploration in science by providing children with science-related tools and materials that complement class themes or existing work. In many cases, a science station is set up on a small table—often in a corner—and designed for only one or two children to use at a time. This arrangement prevents the collaboration and group discussion that characterizes scientific knowledge building. See chapter 4 for more on the important role of discourse.

Gardening provides many opportunities for life science investigations.

Early childhood classrooms often have magnifiers and natural objects for children to investigate.

All too often the items in a science station go unnoticed, or the children's engagement with them is limited to a few minutes here and there. In some cases, the materials available lack a clear connection to the everyday experiences of children. This leaves children little time or interest to investigate things more deeply. Although many teachers are committed to rotating and replacing items frequently to keep things fresh and interesting, that is often where the science ends. Whether they lack knowledge about the basic phenomena the science materials introduce or they lack interest in science as a discipline, many teachers simply don't focus much on science. Even when they do, they sometimes present it as "once and done" activities from a curriculum kit or as an occasional experiment designed more to elicit oohs and aahs rather than to give children tools to build knowledge or deepen their understanding.

Unfortunately, in the primary years science is also often an afterthought. While some well-resourced schools have science specialists or designated times for science within kindergarten and the early grades, this is still quite rare. Many public schools dedicate a majority of time to other disciplines. Standardized science tests don't begin until third grade in many schools, and many districts have a heavy focus on testing, so science is often not taught in the earlier grades to ensure that teachers have enough time to address the subjects that are on the standardized tests.

Since many teachers aren't comfortable with science because they lack the knowledge or interest, they often feel unable to provide science experiences that will be meaningful or fun for their students. In addition, with so many competing demands for time in the primary grades, it can be easy for teachers to make science education a low priority. However, when teachers recognize children's natural curiosity and interest in scientific phenomena, they are often pleased to know they can help them pursue important practices of learning and doing science simply by being intentional about asking questions, supporting children's investigations, and being willing to learn together.

SCIENCE PRACTICES

Have you heard the phrase "Children are natural scientists"? This common observation refers to children's natural curiosity, tendency to ask questions, and seemingly insatiable desire to explore and try things out. In many ways children's natural tendencies and ways of being in the world are very similar to the ways that scientists in all fields do their work. Scientists make careful observations about the world around them, and those observations often lead to questions. They explore and investigate those questions and test their ideas using materials or models, they draw conclusions based on what they've observed or experienced, and they often clarify or change their questions as they go. They share their questions, ideas, and findings with their colleagues and peers. Their discoveries, conversations, and experiences often lead to additional questions and investigations. Sound familiar? To anyone who works with young children, this process is an apt description of how young children learn and engage with the world around them. Even in infancy, children's desire to explore and make meaning from experience drives them to learn and discover their world.

The science education community generally agrees that all people should know and be able to perform particular practices associated with science. While the practices listed below may become more complex or nuanced as children get older, they fundamentally remain the same and thus can be introduced at any age if presented appropriately.

Children investigate a hole in the ice on a frozen puddle.

Asking questions, making observations, and defining problems.

Children engage in this practice when they express curiosity about something they want to explore. Questioning is one of the hallmarks of early childhood, since young people, like scientists, are so driven by their innate curiosity. "Why are all the ducks in that one section of the pond?" would be a typical expression of a child's curiosity about ducks and their behavior. In early childhood, asking questions is closely related to making observations. Children make observations constantly, and these observations usually lead to questions. In early childhood, "defining problems" often looks like children identifying something that they want to investigate (such as the ducks in this example). As children get older, they are often more detailed in their articulation of what it is they want to investigate, learn more about, or explore. Defining problems is also a common practice in the field of engineering, described later in this chapter. Again, since there is so much overlap among the STEM disciplines, a practice identified as fundamental to one area may also be important in another.

Developing and using models or making representations. As learners age and develop, their use of models will grow and become more complex, but in early childhood, models can be as simple as drawings and sketches, representations such as clay figures, stories, and even dramatic play scenarios that help children express their understanding of phenomena or questions. Marta, the child who observed and expressed interest in the ducks during a walk to the park may still be thinking about them later on that day when she makes a representation—she creates a family of ducks out of clay and brings it to the water table to "bring them to the pond." In doing so, she is demonstrating her understanding of the ducks; that they were a family, and that they were in the pond. Marta may even show some mathematical thinking by remembering how many ducks there were (perhaps having counted them when she was outside) and then creating the same number of ducks out of clay.

Planning and carrying out investigations. Children actively seek answers to their own questions by devising ways to investigate them. Marta may try to answer her question about why the ducks are in the pond by observing them for a while to see what they do. She may whoop and holler or wave her arms to see if she can provoke them to move, which would help her better understand their behavior. She might ask her friends what they think, or she might call to the ducks or toss leaves toward them to see their reaction. These are all ways that she investigates her question and the objects of her curiosity. All of the information that she gathers through these actions provide her with data or evidence that she will use to make meaning.

Analyzing and interpreting data. This practice may sound a bit complicated for young children, but it's not. It just means that children use the information that they have gathered through experience or observation to construct knowledge or make meaning about certain phenomena, questions, or observations and to develop their understanding. Going back to our friend Marta at the pond, she has gathered data about the ducks through waving, calling out to them, observing them, and tossing leaves to them. While she may not be recording the data by writing it down, she is remembering it and will draw on it later to make meaning. She might also make observations about the section of the pond the ducks are in, noting that plants are growing at the water's edge. Once she feels she has a sufficient amount of information, she will analyze it and interpret it; that is, she will take all the feedback she received (what the ducks did in response to her provocations) and interpret it to create an explanation about what they were doing and why.

Using mathematics and computational thinking. These science practices are large domains that cover a lot of different ways of thinking! Essentially, they refer to the ability to apply mathematical understanding to a situation, problem, or phenomena. As you will see, young children demonstrate mathematical thinking in many ways, including through their use of patterns, symmetry, relationships, counting, and more. Computational thinking refers to a way of understanding a problem, identifying possible solutions or ways around a problem, and creating ways to respond to the problem. Perhaps most importantly, computational thinking includes the ability to order processes and systems into logical progressions or steps. This linear progression does not usually happen explicitly in early childhood; however, children can often articulate steps of solving a problem after the fact. For example, Marta may not have been able to articulate in advance how she planned to investigate the ducks, but once she had completed a few investigations (waving her arms, throwing leaves), she would likely be able to explain to the teacher how and why she did those things and how the ducks responded.

Constructing explanations and designing solutions. This practice overlaps significantly with using mathematics and computational thinking. When children have gathered and interpreted data based on their investigations, they are able to construct explanations based on what they have seen and experienced. If a teacher asks Marta to tell her why the ducks are in that one section of the pond before she has had a chance to do some investigating, Marta might struggle to explain, or might come up with something arbitrarily. But once she's had a chance to investigate the ducks and collect some data through observation, seeing that they seem to be busy feeding among the plants, she can better explain what she deems to be true about their behavior. Designing solutions refers to children's desire to solve problems or meet challenges. They do this in myriad ways, from coming up with solutions to problems to designing objects or tools to meet certain needs, to developing plans together to aid investigations.

Engaging in argument from evidence. When a person looks at the available evidence or data gathered through investigation, analyzes and interprets that evidence, and then uses it to back up his idea or claim, he is engaging in argument based on evidence. For example, Marta, having undertaken an investigation of "why the ducks are all in that one section of the pond" engages in a discussion with a friend who maintains that they are there because "that's where their house is." Based on her observations and investigation, Marta believes they are there because they like to nibble on the plants growing at the water's edge. She uses her evidence—the data gathered through investigation and observation—to make her point. She has gone through a process of obtaining, evaluating, and communicating information, another key practice in the area of science.

Children at the edge of a pond look for wildlife.

If you watch young children carefully, you will see that they are almost constantly engaged in one or more of these practices. Of course, children will engage in these practices differently depending on their age and development. Why is recognizing and acknowledging these practices essential? While in the past, content was thought to be the most important thing that children could learn, educators now understand that engaging in STEM, as well as understanding and developing comfort and fluency with these practices, is critical because it helps develop and nurture thinking skills with which children construct knowledge for years to come.

Although the terms *practices* and *process skills* might seem to be interchangeable, I prefer the term *practices* when describing the actions and habits associated with doing STEM. Numerous national organizations, such as the National Research Council, the National Council of Teachers of Mathematics, and the National Academies of Science, Engineering, and Medicine, have all in recent years supplanted the term *process skills* with *practices*. This change acknowledges that these ways of approaching and engaging in STEM are more " habits of mind" or thinking patterns than specific, discrete skills that can be taught in isolation.

Particularly in early childhood, these habits of mind are patterns and habits that are being established, and the verb *practice* supports that definition. Finally, I like *practice* because it suggests that one is never quite "done" with developing the habits of mind to which they refer. Just as people need to practice and refine their ability to play a musical instrument, they also need to continue to engage in these practices to refine their understanding and construct knowledge about the world around them.

This child is making observations and collecting data about water and how it moves.

Why Are These Practices Important?

Recognizing and supporting children's use of these practices is critically important. Why? For one thing, the practices listed above are the very same practices that all scientists use in all domains. Science is a way in which we make meaning and understand our world, and our understanding is always evolving and changing as more scientific ideas and questions are investigated. When young children engage in these practices, they are not pretending to be scientists; they *are* being scientists.

Science educator Wynne Harlen noted that children are motivated to learn more when they are empowered and supported (2006). When children have the opportunity to engage in science, they learn to trust their own observations, to value their own questions, and to develop and use the resources at hand to investigate things that are of interest to them. When a caring and intentional adult provides them with the support they need to do so, they feel empowered and confident. They also use the results of their investigations to build their own scientific understanding of the world.

Finally, most people who claim they "don't like science" had negative experiences with science as children. Most likely, they had teachers who were very content focused and perhaps even boring. Perhaps they never had a chance to engage deeply in the practices, being led by curiosity and a desire to understand the world. If we can shift our thinking about science and recognize it for the approachable, joyful, exciting, and interactive discipline it is, we contribute to the development of a generation of people who are confident explorers, full of questions and curiosity.

A rocky shoreline by a shallow pond invites investigation and exploration.

HOW TO SUPPORT CHILDREN'S SCIENCE LEARNING

While the first and most important thing for educators to do is to start to recognize children's questions and engagement in the practices of science, it is also important to have some content knowledge. Content knowledge about basic science concepts and phenomena will help you feel more confident in your abilities to help children make sense of things through their investigations. In appendix A, you will find some of my favorite resources for boosting your own science understanding.

Here are some basic scientific topics that are appropriate and important for early learning. All of these concepts can be introduced in a developmentally appropriate way, and all can be investigated by children in hands-on ways, out of doors. See appendix B for a more complete list, along with suggestions on things you can do outdoors to provoke investigation in these areas.

Technology

When asked to think about technology, most of us can quickly name our favorite digital gizmos and devices—they are ubiquitous in our culture today. But the term *technology* refers to more than just digital technology. It includes the knowledge and understanding of all tools or mechanisms—any tool that humans use. When considered in this way, how we think about technology in early childhood becomes much broader and far-reaching. For example, pencils, tape, and even shoes are technology. *Technology* refers to objects created by humans to serve specific purposes. Considering technology in these terms sheds a new light on the way we consider integrating technology in the classroom, the way we talk about it, use it, and make meaning with it. In early childhood settings, most adults use the terms *tools* and *technology* interchangeably because they are the same thing. Although we tend first to think of digital media and devices as technology, particularly with young children, we should consider all tools to be technology. Still, digital technology is a prominent feature of the educational landscape. It can be a powerful and potent tool for learning, both inside and outside of the classroom. Countless apps, games, educational programs, and other resources are available, many of which claim to enhance learning.

These boys use a common kitchen scale to weigh a rock.

Technology in the early childhood setting can take the form of any tool or object that is used for a specific purpose, but young children should have opportunities to use tools and technology *in the service of their learning*. We want children to use technology to deepen their understanding, to help them make observations, to answer questions, to gather information, and to help them design solutions to problems or challenges. We also want them to use technology to help them express their ideas and understanding about the world. We encourage them to use it to make meaning from their experiences. These experiences are the very practices of science, engineering, and mathematics that we want to support in early childhood.

While many educators reject the notion that digital media is appropriate for early childhood settings, others believe that with intention and careful planning, teachers can help children use digital media in service of learning. To do so, teachers need to know how to critically evaluate digital tools and media and carefully balance their use and ensure they are clearly connected to learning, not just making children passive consumers of media. Teachers need to know how to support children in learning to use media to create things, make art, communicate, and play. Teachers also need to understand how to help children think critically about what they are seeing and doing with digital media. This is a way of bringing technology integration into the realm of inquiry (described below) rather than simply rote skill building or consumption of media. Teachers can also support critical thinking when they engage with children and media in the service of learning and the spirit of inquiry.

Digital cameras are a popular way to use technology during outdoor explorations.

TYPICAL TECHNOLOGY IN AN EARLY CHILDHOOD CLASSROOM

What tools do early learners use to make meaning from their experiences—particularly those involving science, engineering, and math? They use art tools, such as markers, paintbrushes, glue, tape, pens, pencils, and crayons, to express themselves and make meaning from their experiences. They use tools such as shovels, spoons, scoops, measuring cups, boxes, and jars to move and measure materials. They use scales, measuring tapes, yarn, rulers, and ribbon to measure and better understand objects and distances. They use calendars, clocks, and sundials to measure time. They use magnifiers and binoculars to examine objects near and far. They use digital cameras to document their findings. They may use apps for drawing or writing down their ideas and collecting data. They may use mapping software or programs to see bird's-eye views of the places where they live and play. Teachers may show videos or video clips from the Internet to introduce children to new ideas, to expose them to places they may never have been, or to share information about other animals, environments, and cultures to increase their awareness of the world around them.

Technology use in early childhood settings includes the tools and materials children use to make sense of the world.

The early childhood setting has many types of technology and ways to use them. Early childhood educators should seek out and utilize only developmentally appropriate resources and strategies that support environmental *and* technology literacy. The vast array of tools and materials available to children can help them gain environmental literacy through engaging them in outdoor exploration. Digital technology in the early childhood classroom can also contribute to young children's knowledge construction because it allows young children to represent, organize, and communicate their ideas using another medium, and it provides tools and strategies for them to visualize and reflect on their learning (Hong and Trepanier-Street 2004).

RECOMMENDATIONS FOR DEVELOPMENTALLY APPROPRIATE USES OF TECHNOLOGY

In response to the maelstrom of information and available resources on children's media use, the Fred Rogers Center for Early Learning and Children's Media at St. Vincent College, and the National Association for the Education of Young Children (NAEYC) developed a position statement on the use of technology and media in early childhood classrooms, which was designed to help educators think critically about how to approach children's use of digital media and technology (see appendix A). The NAEYC/Fred Rogers Center statement cautions educators to apply their knowledge of developmentally appropriate practice and pedagogy to this new world of digital media:

> Teachers must take the time to evaluate and select technology and media for the classroom, carefully observe children's use of the materials to identify opportunities and problems, and then make appropriate adaptations. They must be willing to learn about and become familiar with new technologies as they are introduced and be intentional in the choices they make, including ensuring that content is developmentally appropriate and that it communicates anti-bias messages. (2012, 6)

In addition, content should be inclusive of all children, regardless of physical or cognitive ability, ethnic background, or socioeconomic status. It is important to

All children deserve to feel safe and secure in the natural world.

consider not just developmentally appropriate content, but anti-bias messages and subject matter. Strive for inclusion and cultural competence in your STEM-related media resources. Seek out media that reflect different cultures and approaches to learning STEM. Find material that represents children of all ethnic backgrounds and ability levels, and from nontraditional families. Ensure that diverse populations are represented in any media you use to explore STEM, because all children need to see themselves represented in those fields. For anti-bias resources, refer to appendix A.

Educators who have a vested interest in connecting children to nature or to teaching outdoors may also want to consider the impact of media messages about nature and the environment. Such messages are powerful and can impact young children in subtle yet significant ways. Considering the messages that media portrayals of nature, animals, and humans' relationship to the natural world send to young children is useful. The opportunity to use technology to deepen children's relationships to the natural world is a powerful and exciting one, so consider the many ways in which media portrayals of nature and animals can be interpreted and ensure that the messages conveyed are positive and affirming. As I wrote in my book *Early Childhood Activities for a Greener Earth*, it's worth seeking out books and stories that have positive messages about humans, animals, and the natural world. Many books present nature in a less-than-positive light or present animals as villains or aggressive creatures. Many books, even those that purport to be "environmentally focused," also present humans as destructive toward the natural world, offering a bleak or hopeless view of the future. I believe that children should be exposed to literature and even nonfiction books that portray the natural world as a safe, joyful place where children are free to live, grow, and learn.

CHALLENGES IN USING TECHNOLOGY

The 2010 report *Always Connected: The New Digital Media Habits of Young Children* indicated that preschool and primary-grade children typically consume between four and eight hours of media each day (Gutnick, Robb, Takeuchi, and Kotler). Given this reality, many educators understandably express concern that digital technology will replace the critical hands-on experiences that are so important in early childhood: moving and exploring, manipulating objects, engaging in dramatic play, creating and building, and forming relationships with others. Others contend that digital technology should be embraced because it provides opportunities for differentiated instruction, formative assessment, playful learning, and student engagement. Finding the right balance is tricky. The resources in appendix A can provide help.

Admittedly, it's hard to keep up with all the new developments in technology, much less evaluate them for developmental appropriateness, and to build a thorough understanding of the benefits and consequences of digital technology in the early years. At the time of this writing, over a thousand new apps are being created each day (Pocketgamer.biz 2017). Add to that the large number of digital media organizations and corporations that offer commercial products geared toward early childhood, and it's hard to know how to make sense of it all. Of course, it's imperative that educators who wish to use technology in their classrooms—whether preschool or primary grade—ensure that the technology is designed and used to enhance those hands-on learning experiences rather than replace them. As noted above, technology should be used in the service of children's learning. Regardless of how much or how little digital media you choose to implement, you will also want to be aware of considerations around violence, stereotypes in media, educational value, and overall developmental appropriateness.

ACCESSIBILITY AND INCLUSION

While the increased use of digital technology presents a risk that some children with physical disabilities or low/impaired vision or hearing may be left out of the learning opportunity, assistive technology makes it possible for these

Assistive technology can help ensure that all children can be included in outdoor learning.

children to participate alongside their peers. In this way, digital media offers unique opportunities for learning: the variety of accessible digital media that is designed for children who have physical disabilities is growing at a rapid pace. The world of assistive technology includes features such as voice recognition, screen readers and magnifiers, adaptive keyboards, and more. These features allow children who otherwise may not have been able to participate to engage with digital media for learning. As they do with other classroom tools, teachers who use digital technology in the classroom should be committed to seeking out only those tools that offer accessibility features in order to ensure that all children can participate.

Many teachers also see the potential of digital technology to offer educational benefits to young children of all ability levels. With the enormous variety of apps and educational software available, many teachers see digital technology as a way to expand opportunities for learning and are eager to try new things. Assistive technology goes beyond digital technology as well. A vast array of equipment is available to help teachers create access to outdoor places for children with physical impairments. See http://headstartinclusion.org for suggestions. The Office of Head Start is a good place to get started learning more about modifications for children with physical or other limitations. Check your own state's Department of Health and Human Services or some of the resources in appendix A.

THE PRACTICES OF TECHNOLOGY LITERACY

How do young children demonstrate fluency with technology? What are the thinking skills associated with technology in the early years? While many adults can share experiences of toddlers who know how to tap and swipe a digital device to find an app, the technology that I'm referring to here is the use of any tools in service of learning, which is a significant distinction.

The National Association for Media Literacy Education (NAMLE) considers "habits of inquiry" and "skills of expression" as two touchstones of media and technology literacy for young children. The NAMLE suggests these are foundational skills that will help children develop such literacy as they grow. For very young children, NAMLE suggests the following practices.

Children learn to use media to express themselves creatively when they write and draw outdoors.

Habits of Inquiry

Questioning, decision making, and integration—these are practices that children engage in constantly in all of the STEM disciplines. When it comes to media and technology, watch how they engage with media, including technology, books, and magazines. For example, media may inspire children to create and identify questions of their own, things they wonder about that they wish to better understand. It may provoke questions like "What is going to happen next?" during a read-aloud, or "Why does that bird have such long legs?" when looking at a picture book. Their questions might relate to the technology itself: "Why does the computer make that sound when I turn it on?" or "How does this game work?" This active questioning suggests that children are using media as a springboard for their own curiosity and wonder.

Questioning about technology and tools also helps children think through their use of more traditional nondigital tools. Technology-related questioning often serves as a direct pathway into engineering, since children often respond to their own questions with ideas about how to solve problems; for example, "How can I get these marbles out of the bottle?" or "How can I make a raft for my army guys to float across the puddle?" The child's natural response is to evaluate the tools available, select the best one for the job, or create something new.

Children demonstrate a capacity for media- and technology-related decision making as well. They do this often, such as when they create labels, signs, and pictures for their personal cubby area or their place at the table, and when they write shopping lists or address envelopes in the writing center. They also demonstrate decision making when they create books or stories, choose subjects for photos and drawings, and represent objects or situations through writing or scribbling. They make decisions about what kind of media and technology to use and how best to represent their thoughts and ideas. This decision making naturally overlaps with media integration, which they demonstrate when they choose how to use media in the service of learning, or how they choose to communicate or process their ideas, thoughts, and questions.

Children often make decisions about which tools to use for what purpose and how to use tools in new and innovative ways. In doing so, they allude to their underlying knowledge about structure, function, and properties of materials.

STEM Start

If a child, Mateo, is digging in hard soil with a plastic shovel that breaks, he might select the next nearest tool to continue digging the hole. He reaches for a small rake but quickly becomes frustrated at having to use it to try to dig. He sets the rake aside and reaches for a large metal spoon, which is a better digging tool, but it makes the work go much more slowly.

By observing Mateo's behavior and engaging in a conversation about his tool selection, the teacher can learn more about what he knows about certain tools and why some work better than others. She can ask him what features of the shovel make it a good digging tool and why the rake is not so good for that purpose. She can also elicit his understanding of the similarities between the spoon and the shovel and what makes them better tools than the rake for this job. She can ask him how he might make the job go faster even though the best tool to use is the spoon, which makes the job go much more slowly than the shovel did. In his responses, Mateo will talk about the tools, but he will likely also describe the soil he is trying to move and how the texture of the soil factors into his decisions about tool selection. This demonstrates an awareness of the properties of soil, and the teacher can go one step further by asking him if he knows of any way he could change the soil to make it less hard.

This boy uses tools to move soil and mud from one place to another.

Children demonstrate an awareness of integration of technology when they seek out and use media or technology for their own purposes. For example, when a child is curious about a bird outside, she may go to a bookshelf to find a bird book, she may ask the teacher to look on the computer for more information about that bird, or she may draw or write about birds. In this example, she is demonstrating an awareness of the integration of media, both digital and otherwise. Any time a child demonstrates knowledge that there is a tool or resource that will help her learn something or accomplish her outcome, she practices integration. The ability to access or create those integrated resources is something that develops over time, and again, teachers can help children articulate that understanding by asking plenty of questions about their plans or ideas for accessing or creating solutions.

Children make decisions about the kind of media that will help them in their investigations.

Math and Computational Thinking

When children engage in the act of creating technology, they are engaging in math and computational thinking. Rather than simply being consumers of media, young children can interact with some digital technology that lets them create media such as games and images, or stop-motion video. *Computational thinking* is described as the process of identifying a problem, then designing and representing a solution that can be carried out by a computer (Cuny, Snyder and Wing 2010). Research by Douglas H. Clements and Julie Sarama indicates that digital applications that engage children in spatial and mathematical thinking (such as manipulating objects in space, rotating and changing the position of items) can help children build awareness and deepen spatial understanding (2004).

Some primary grades teachers have started to implement computer coding in the classroom to help children learn the language of computers. Children can use simple, intuitive websites and apps to learn to write computer programs such as Scratch, the computer programming language developed by the Lifelong Kindergarten Group at the Massachusetts Institute of Technology Media Lab. In Scratch, children can simply "click and drag" commands that visually fit together like puzzle pieces. This helps children get a sense of how certain commands work together and how to create certain actions on the computer, such as moving an image across the screen or designing a simple video game. Some coding programs (including Scratch) are designed for the very young, with visually stimulating, intuitive sequences of activities and plenty of feedback. Most others are designed for older children, for whom this activity is more developmentally appropriate.

Some early elementary settings use programmable robots to help children learn about Boolean thinking—that is, thinking that is black-and-white, either/or, logical. This is fun and engaging for many children and supports computational thinking, as described above. These skills also help children refine their thinking and inquiry abilities because they learn to think about and express the steps and processes in very specific, linear ways. See appendix A for resources on coding and robotics activities.

Skills of Expression, Communication, and Representation

Representation is an important skill in the domains of science, engineering, and mathematics. In early learning, this is also called modeling. Representation is essentially a way of expressing ideas or concepts in ways that can be understood by others. When you give children access to a variety of tools, materials, and, yes, media in which to represent their understanding, they will have more freedom to express themselves creatively and to share their learning and understanding with others.

Rather than simply serving as a source of information that children consume, appropriate use of digital technology can help older, primary-grade children become producers of material via blogs, newsletters, reports, collages, games, wikis, and videos, all of which helps them to make meaning from their experience. It allows them to articulate and communicate their understanding and knowledge with their peers, which is how technology is used in the science, engineering, and math disciplines. It is also used in STEM disciplines for record keeping, so helping elementary-aged learners use computers to manage data or record activities is appropriate.

Primary-grade students can create group websites or blogs about their work or presentations with computer applications. These products enable young people to collaborate on the creation and the presentation of the material to their peers and even their families. Young children can print photos taken with digital cameras and type descriptions of their investigations or experiences. Children in the primary grades often enjoy using loose parts to create stop-motion videos or time-lapse photography of natural phenomena.

In any case, when considering how to engage children in using technology to document their learning and discoveries, remember that technology should be used in the service of children's learning. Digital technology that reduces activity and experience to rote memorization, that limits thinking to activities like selecting answers from a list rather than posing open-ended questions, or activities that serve as nothing more than "digital worksheets" should be avoided. While digital technology is ubiquitous and a part of even the youngest children's everyday lives, technology can never compare to the value of authentic, hands-on experiences in nature. Children should be engaged in outdoor learning and using real materials for learning whenever possible.

USING TECHNOLOGY OUTDOORS

Teachers can use digital media and technology in many ways to engage children in explorations of the natural world, provided they use them as extensions of hands-on experiences and investigation. But remember that firsthand, direct experience with the natural world is preferred whenever possible. Many teachers use digital cameras, video recordings, or scanners to photograph and save images from outdoor excursions and investigations. Digital documentation can be a fun reminder of outdoor experiences, and documentation, representation, and communication are key STEM practices, so engaging students with media in a way that supports the development of these skills can be useful.

Webcams are exciting and bring children live-feed images of animals in zoos or their natural habitats, and there are even webcams that focus on natural features such as volcanoes and other weather events. I once worked with a first-grade class that checked their "owl cam" every day as part of their morning routine. A nature center hundreds of miles to the north of the school had a live camera feed trained on a nesting owl. During snacktime in the classroom, the teacher pulled up the owl cam on the digital whiteboard so the children could make observations and discuss owl behavior. When the eggs finally hatched, the children were able to see the fuzzy owlets growing and developing. If your school has the resources, you may even consider setting up a live webcam at your bird-feeding station, or school garden, or in a grove of nearby trees. As much excitement as webcams may bring to the classroom, however, please remember that hands-on experiences in nature are better whenever possible.

There are apps designed to help people learn birdsongs and birdcalls, as well as other wildlife sounds, which can delight and inspire children (and teachers) who are developing an interest in birds and other wildlife. A number of high-quality insect and plant identification apps exist for those who are interested in learning the names of local species.

Some teachers like to bring students outdoors with a specific purpose in mind, such as doing fieldwork like counting animals, tracking bloom time for plants, or simply taking phenology notes. Upon returning indoors, the class records the data they have collected on a website that gathers information from other "citizen scientists" across the country. Several citizen science websites are

Note: When using birdcalls or wildlife sounds during outdoor explorations, please consider migration and nesting season, as well as the territorial needs of animals. Birdcalls should only be used occasionally and after consideration. See appendix A for a link to recommendations for using bird calls responsibly.

appropriate and enjoyable for young children. Among the best are Cornell Lab of Ornithology's citizen science Project FeederWatch, which engages children in making simple observations of common birds. Children in classrooms in any state or region identify species, track prevalence, and even make observations about the health and relative abundance of certain species of common birds. Scientists and resource managers around the country use the data entered on this website to learn more about bird populations, invasive species, bird behavior, and health issues that affect birds.

Even the youngest students can participate in citizen science projects, and in doing so, they develop their skills of observation, data collection and analysis, counting, measuring, order of operations, representation, and interpretation of information. Many teachers report that citizen science "helps make science real" because children learn the value of careful observation and record keeping. Knowing that the information is being used for scientific purposes helps children understand the importance of accurate data collection. It can also contribute to a sense of classroom community and environmental responsibility because children know that their field observations are contributing to the larger scientific community. These types of citizen science projects can also be great jumping-off points for additional investigations (see appendix A for more suggestions).

Digital technology is here to stay. Educators who approach the issue thoughtfully, with clear objectives for how technology will be used to enhance and supplement children's outdoor investigations, are sure to find something that meets their needs.

Engineering

So much of what young children are fascinated by and interested in involves designing and creating things: costumes, houses, stores, block structures, and homes for their toys. Young children love to create purposeful tools of their own design for their play. In this case, the "tools" are the structures and homes they create to support their own play. These are things usually constructed out of blocks or other materials provided in the classroom. I refer to them as tools because they are components of children's play that children create to serve their own needs.

In real life, engineers use a variety of tools to design and develop solutions to problems. There are all kinds of engineers, and most people's lives are made better by the work of engineers. Some engineers work with machines, such as developing cars that are lighter and more aerodynamic to save on fuel and reduce emissions. Some engineers work with chemicals, designing and refining medicines or using chemistry to help other scientists do their work. Some engineers are electrical engineers, planning out and designing electrical systems for homes, buildings, even cities. Civil engineers work with buildings and homes too, developing and planning street systems and water management systems, or planning other types of development. Other engineers work in the field of medicine, developing prosthetic limbs or other medical devices to help people achieve years of health and freedom. Still other types of engineers develop software systems on which our banks and other commerce systems depend. There is no shortage of ways in which the work of engineers helps us to live better lives. Engineering helps us develop solutions to many of our problems and meet our needs.

Many opportunities are available to introduce engineering into the world of the young child. In the classroom, block play is where most educators can observe children as they enthusiastically create and rebuild structures, systems of ramps and pathways, marble runs, and towers again and again. Building and creating are common ways that young children engage in one part of the process of engineering. Consider this example: Using box–shaped cardboard blocks, three boys try to make a tower taller than the tallest boy in the group. Stacking the blocks one on top of another, however, challenges them, because as the tower grows taller, it also becomes less steady. Despite the fact that the tower continues to fall, they return to their creation again and again for nearly thirty minutes, attempting to refine their design to keep it from crashing down.

While most early childhood classrooms have dedicated block areas, and examples like the one above may occur on an almost daily basis, remember that simply building in the block area does not necessarily mean that children are engaging in engineering. Of course, building is a fundamental first step in engineering, and children often set out in their building with a clear goal in mind, but there is more to engineering than block building alone. Hidden inside this open-ended block play is actually a series of steps that reflects the work of engineers.

The boys have identified a problem that they want to solve and have begun to

Children love to build large-scale creations outdoors, such as the shelter made by this boy and his friends.

address it together. By experimenting with different stacking configurations and a variety of blocks, they are learning about properties of the blocks they are using, including weight, size, and shape. They are also exploring balance, structures, and strength as they try to create a tower that won't tumble down. Engineering happens outdoors as well. Children love to build and create things out of materials they find. Often, educators find that children's engineering play is longer in duration and more creative when it takes place outdoors, involving a variety of diverse pieces and parts with different properties, such as texture, heft, size, and shape.

DESIGN THINKING SKILLS

Young children are naturally inclined to engage in engineering-related activities, and they take part in engineering practices with some regularity. Within this context of planning, designing, building, and testing, children refine their thinking skills, learn to collaborate, develop a sense of persistence, and learn to see things in many ways. Engineering gives young children a context in which to explore, create things, try things out, and redesign things. It suits their natural inclination to persist at tasks until they successfully reach a given outcome. It can also contribute to skills of self-regulation, collaboration, and creative thinking.

The engineering design process can be a useful way to approach engineering education with young children. The engineering design process refers to the process by which engineers confront a problem or challenge. It includes a few discrete steps, including developing an idea, designing a solution or plan, testing that solution, and redesigning it to improve the solution. As you can see, within that process, some of the practices described in the section on science (specifically defining problems, planning, and designing solutions) are also important to the discipline of engineering.

In the graphic on the next page, note that a range of steps or phases are identified. Different organizations and educators identify them slightly differently. Like nature play and nature immersion, you can think of the engineering design process as a spectrum.

The engineering design process is usually defined as having specific steps. Although it is described as a process and is often represented as a cycle, remember that in early childhood, the process is seldom linear or discrete. Children move from one phase to the next and back again throughout their work and play. They may engage more deeply and for longer periods during one phase or another.

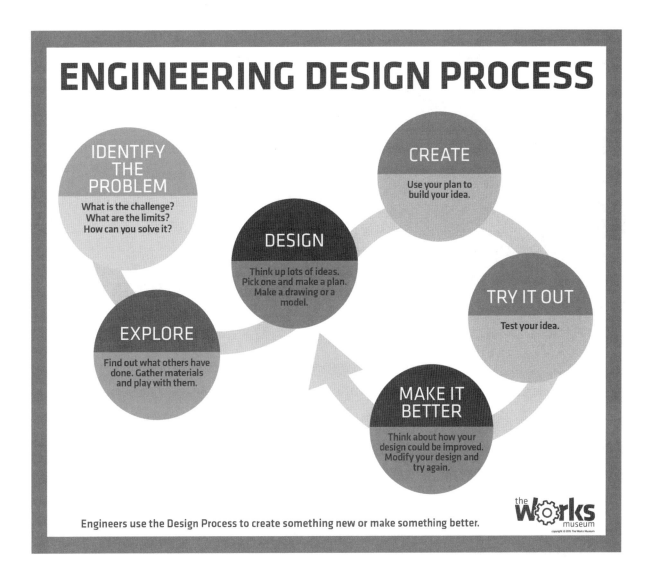

ENGINEERING DESIGN PROCESS

IDENTIFY THE PROBLEM
What is the challenge?
What are the limits?
How can you solve it?

CREATE
Use your plan to build your idea.

DESIGN
Think up lots of ideas. Pick one and make a plan. Make a drawing or a model.

TRY IT OUT
Test your idea.

EXPLORE
Find out what others have done. Gather materials and play with them.

MAKE IT BETTER
Think about how your design could be improved. Modify your design and try again.

Engineers use the Design Process to create something new or make something better.

the **Works** museum
copyright © 2015 The Works Museum

The first step in the process is developing or having an idea or merely asking a question ("I want to make a house for my stuffed cat"). When young children make observations about a problem, opportunity, or need, it is usually accompanied by thinking about, imagining, and dreaming up solutions. The natural progression in the process is creating that idea through design, or planning out the solution. Usually for young children, a design is a mental picture or a particular idea of what the item will be. For older children this may be a sketch or even a conversation about what they want to create. In early childhood, design often happens in tandem with the planning phase, and children constantly move in and out of the plan, design, and build phases as they are working on their creations.

These girls discuss their ideas for building a structure out of sticks.

Next comes building the item (constructing it out of blocks, boxes, or other materials). Young children usually "design as they go," making alterations to their creations while in progress, refining their ideas as they work collaboratively with one another. Their process also usually involves a test of the design (which might be as simple as putting the cat in the house to see if it fits!). This stage is especially important in engineering because it is when children determine if their creations have worked as planned—whether they have served the intended purpose. When children test their creations, they get immediate feedback on their design. If things don't work as planned, they reflect on the design of the creation or the structure and consider what to change. If necessary, the child will redevelop or alter the design; for example, if the doorway is too small for the cat to fit through, the child may change the arrangement of blocks to make the opening wider.

At its core, the engineering design process generally follows this progression, but there will be exceptions. As you observe children engaging in engineering, try to identify how and when they engage in the different phases.

Educators often include communicating as a key component of the engineering design process to help children articulate the results of their work. Describing one's thinking is a powerful way for children to reflect on their plan, their design, and any improvements they made. It can also be a good way for teachers to learn more about their students' understanding of the properties of materials they have used, as well as their understanding of concepts like structures, scale, and size.

With intentionality, teachers can help older children understand the process of engineering as well as what engineers do and the challenges they face. While the goal is not to get children to think about what they want to be when they grow up, helping young children understand the role of engineers in society can help them identify as engineers. Normalizing engineering by talking about it as a job and as a profession of helping others (by designing solutions to problems) can help children develop an interest in the field. Within the field of engineering, whether chemical, mechanical, structural, or some other kind of engineering, there are numerous opportunities for creativity, helping others, and improving lives. Helping children see these possibilities is important in establishing a personal interest and connection to the discipline.

ENGINEERING HABITS OF MIND

Have you ever watched a child building a block tower and been tempted to tell her how to make a steady base or straighten out the blocks so it doesn't tumble down? It's tempting because we want to see the child reach a successful conclusion. But it's particularly important—in fact, in engineering it is critical—to have designs *not* work as planned at times, to let them fail. It is during these times that children are prompted to think critically about materials, the building/creating process, and the choices they have made in creating. That is when they have the opportunity to refine their thinking, change their plans, and try again. As you will see, there are a number of social-emotional benefits to engaging in the practices of engineering, as well as a great deal of cognitive growth that occurs. Additionally, when children have opportunities to fail while building or creating, they are more likely to gain comfort with it and to be more resilient when they face failure in the future. Engineering affords children the opportunity to practice perseverance and persistence. When a teacher helps children see the value in failure through the lessons it teaches, children can view failure in a whole new light. Consider all the useful information that can be gained when things don't go as planned. In addition to providing opportunities to learn about materials, structures, and systems, engineering practices also help children develop social and intrapersonal skills.

In 2009 a group of educators articulated a set of six habits of mind particular to engineering, including systems thinking, creativity, optimism, collaboration, communication, and attention to ethical considerations (Katehi et al. 2009). Again we see the overlap between the thinking and practices associated with engineering and those of the disciplines of science, technology, and mathematics.

Systems thinking is defined as the ability to recognize interconnections. This type of thinking is evident when children design and create marble runs or other elaborate structures. Children begin to grasp interconnection when they realize that moving or changing one element of a system affects the other parts involved. In the classroom, children quickly learn that when one block is removed from a tower, the others sometimes come crashing down.

Children also recognize systems in the natural world. For example, thinking about systems could mean noticing that leaves and branches make up distinct parts of a tree but are also part of the

"Productive struggle" can help children build persistence, an important habit of mind.

Children investigating water and sand build an understanding of water systems.

larger system that is the whole tree. Or it could mean recognizing that streams of water dug into a lake's sandy shoreline flow together to become larger streams that eventually join the lake.

Creativity is evident in children's engineering play from the get-go. Children are endlessly imaginative in the solutions they dream up and the creations they design. Often, the only limit to children's creativity is the resources available to support their ideas! Engineering is a context in which children are able, with freedom and support, to really immerse themselves in creative thinking and acting. And since the natural world is a context in which children tend to demonstrate more creative play (Kahn and Kellert 2002), it makes sense to bring engineering play outside. Providing opportunities for children to engineer in nature-based settings—to build stick forts, construct mud huts, make small worlds, and create pathways through brush and grass—can be a significant creative outlet for young children while also offering them the opportunity to work on a larger scale than they would be able to do indoors, and with a greater diversity of materials.

Optimism is another habit of mind identified as crucial to engineering. Have you ever seen children get fully engaged in something, or stick closely to a task, focusing their attention on it for extended periods of time? As you likely know, children can become deeply immersed in building creations, persisting at building or working regardless of how many times a tower comes crashing down. They often face their frustration head-on, fully expecting to succeed despite any challenges or limitations that may exist. I suggest two more characteristics that are evident when children are engineering: resilience and persistence. These three characteristics—optimism, resilience, and persistence—are closely linked. Not only does failure in engineering create opportunities for persistence in the face of repeated unsuccessful attempts, but persistence indicates a feeling of optimism: the children fully expect to succeed at their task if given enough time. Regardless of how many times that tower falls, some children are determined to keep trying until they are successful at making it stand strong.

Persistence is also evident when children continue looking for and testing materials until they find just the right fit for a structure that has a gap in it. Or they may adjust their construction in particular ways so that it can hold a toy or serve a given purpose (Bandura 2001). When children have freedom and safety to explore and experiment in a classroom community that values risk taking and supports this type of investigation, they develop a sense of self-efficacy, which leads to resilience and persistence. These are among the skills that many early educators aim to nurture in young children, and engineering design explorations offer children a lot of opportunities to develop and "try on" those qualities while also building their own self-confidence.

Children will engage in engineering while working or playing alone, but, as with the other disciplines in STEM, engineering naturally leads to collaboration, which is one of its greatest benefits in the early childhood setting. Children collaborate when they talk with friends about their designs, make plans and think through ideas together, listen to one another, negotiate for materials, and work together on their creations. Children design and engineer solutions while working together on problems or challenges. They might start out with one idea in mind and quickly shift gears, inspired by what someone else is doing or eager to incorporate one friend's idea into their own. They collaborate when they work together to build structures or other creations they have invented as a team.

Engineering activities can also be a great boost to young children's language and literacy development because they require so much communication. Engaging in the active process of engineering together requires children to problem solve, think, and talk through solutions. They make suggestions about improvements to design and provide evidence and reasons for why they believe their ideas will work. Children also learn together when their designs don't work. They try out new vocabulary words, which have a real context, like *balance*, *stable*, *sturdy*, and *foundation*, as they strive to create structures that will stand on their own. For this type of interaction to occur, creating a climate of collaboration is necessary. When children have a space to collaborate and work together, and a classroom where risk taking and teamwork are supported, where they are free to make mistakes and learn alongside their peers, they are more likely to have strong peer-to-peer relationships that are full of discourse and conversation (Maxwell et al. 2008).

Engineering offers a context in which children make authentic ethical decisions (can I share my materials with Haley? How can I walk around that marble run tower without knocking it over?) and wrestle with important inter- and intrapersonal issues. They negotiate with friends for materials and space, and they consider one another's creations and are mindful of safety. Just as professional engineers often have to work within the constraints of limited resources, such as time, materials, and even help from others, children engineering with loose parts demonstrate this capacity as well. When they know time is limited, many children will scramble to finish building their creation before it is time to head indoors for another activity. When materials are limited, children thoughtfully plan how they will use them or will redesign their creations in order to work within those constraints. At times, of course, this is done through trial and error, when children find they have run out of materials before completing their work or that they need to share with friends. Children are challenged to respect one another's space for building and will often take great care to step around their friends' creations.

Children are also challenged to use materials safely, particularly when building outdoors. Long, heavy, or jagged sticks may be the perfect elements for Alaina's fort, but she needs to be aware of the safety of others as she carries and drags the sticks from the forest edge to her worksite. All of this management of resources and awareness of others can be challenging and at times frustrating for young children, but it helps them develop patience, a sense of how to work together, and an understanding of how to distribute, share, and manage limited resources. This sense of ethics and attention to the needs of others is something that professional engineers grapple with as well.

Of course, some children delight in knocking down others' creations, and that also presents opportunities to learn. Seldom done with malicious intent, the act of knocking down a building is usually just one child's innocent attempt to "see what will happen." Even if they have been told time and time again not to knock down others' creations, it's a temptation that is hard to resist. They are curious about how (and if!) the structure will fall, how much pressure or force they need to apply in order to effect a change. If you can look at

Engineers young and old need to be aware of ethical considerations, such as the constraints of space, materials, and the effect of one's actions on others.

this common situation as a learning opportunity for both the builder and the "demolition expert," you can capitalize on children's natural inclinations and respond to hurt feelings with greater understanding. The builders can be prompted to re-create their constructions in new ways or exactly from memory. Acknowledging the "knocker-downer's" curiosity is a way to validate his curiosity, and you can also show respect for the builder's time and effort by creating clear rules and expectations ahead of time. This is a context in which children learn about ethics and respect for others' creations. They learn to practice impulse control and manage their feelings through self-regulation. Recognizing the strong impulse that children have to knock down others' towers, some teachers impose rules such as "ask before knocking"—and sometimes that is all it takes to nip the problem in the bud. Other teachers set up barriers around children's creations to protect them from getting knocked down, and others make a point to respond in a very matter-of-fact way to help children develop resilience and a willingness to try again.

SOURCING MATERIALS

Another important skill involved in the engineering process, particularly with very young children, is sourcing materials. *Sourcing* means finding the appropriate material for a designated purpose. Sourcing materials indoors is something children can do with little effort: the building materials (usually wood blocks, bristle blocks, Lego blocks) are usually located in a certain area of the classroom, and many teachers generally discourage children from using other objects for building, if for no other reason than to control the disarray! Indoors, the building materials are generally pretty uniform and don't challenge children to draw on their prior knowledge about what materials will work best. Classroom building materials become familiar very quickly.

When children are busy outdoors working on creations of their own design and need to source materials, they draw on a different set of skills than when they play with Lego and other blocks from discrete containers. Outdoors, children tap into their spatial reasoning: looking at objects and imagining how they would work in their creations; forming mental images of a variety of objects' shapes, sizes, and proportions; and mentally rotating the objects they see as they scan the ground for appropriate building materials. Children handle and explore all sorts of materials: sticks, stones, sand, mud, leaves, branches, and more. They gather information and build knowledge about scale, weight, size, and shape as they pick up, put down, and select the materials needed to do the job. This understanding of the properties of the building materials they select can only be gained through direct experience.

In natural settings, when children are challenged to identify *for themselves* which materials will be best suited for a certain engineering purpose, as well as how and where to find those materials, they draw on their prior experience with those materials. They also need to think mathematically about the shapes, sizes, and proportions of the materials they are considering. They do this when they estimate and compare materials mentally and by hand. They measure, often "eyeballing it" to see if things will fit together. They draw on their knowledge of properties and attributes of the materials they are considering. Consider one young boy's thinking:

> "Should I use rocks or sticks to make the fence for my fairy house? The rocks are good because they're shiny, but the sticks are long and pointy

and will be harder for the lizards to climb over. But I'm going to need a lot more sticks."

Using Reflection to Support Engineering Learning

Most early educators recognize the curiosity and creativity that young children demonstrate constantly, and these are brought to the forefront when children have building materials and freedom to play and explore. Children require little prompting to become deeply engaged in creative explorations when they have the freedom to invent new creations, design new structures, and create systems (for example, when they create networks of "roads" out of blocks or strips of bark, or when they make fairy structures or other shelters out of natural materials and other loose parts).

Children use care to select the materials that will be just right for their needs.

Just as it takes more than simply building in the block area to create engineering opportunities for children, it's important to offer children more than just a variety of interesting and inspiring materials. To ensure that the children in your class are engaging deeply in engineering, remember a few simple but important things: Asking questions that relate to the different stages of their planning and creating will direct their attention to their choices and prompt them to tell you how they created plans or designs. Also inquire about their choices of materials.

Ask questions such as these about the choices children make to help them further refine their skills in engineering:

> "**What made you choose** the wood planks rather than the leaves when you made that bridge?"
>
> "**How can you make something that will** hold these acorns and keep them dry?"
>
> "I see you are making a bridge to cross over that puddle. **What are you planning to do?**"
>
> "Hmm. It looks like your platform to hold acorns above the forest floor tipped over. It only has two legs. **What do you think you could change** so that it wouldn't tip over?"
>
> "**Tell me about the design** of your fairy house."

"I've noticed these tiny purple flowers here are getting trampled. **What might we design to help** our friends remember to stay on the path?"

These are all questions that gently encourage children to consider the properties of the materials they have selected or to tell you about a plan that they are making, which helps them engage more deeply in the engineering design process.

By bringing their attention to things such as materials, choices, or where their designs "went wrong," and even by posing specific challenges to children, you can ensure that their playful building helps children thoughtfully engage in the process of designing and building. When it comes to engineering in early childhood, remember that children are still building knowledge about the properties of materials, how and why they work, how they can be manipulated and used, and even in natural settings, where to find them. Engineering will be most meaningful for young children when they have opportunities to be intentional about their process and their role in creating things.

To best support children in engaging in the process of engineering, teachers must help bring their attention to what they are doing, how they made their decisions, and how their choices have impacted their creation. They can ask them to describe what they are going to do (what their plan is) and to notice how they test and redesign. Engaging children in this discourse or metacognition (thinking about their own thinking) is a key way to bring their attention to how and what they are doing (VanMeeteren and Zan 2010).

When you observe children at work in the block area or building creations outdoors, you can use a variety of ways to help them deepen their engagement. You might start by asking, "What are you doing?" "How did you decide to do that?" "What materials did you choose for that purpose? Why?" "How did you know that the wide piece of wood would be stronger than that skinny one there?" These are the sorts of questions that will make children think about their choices and their reasons for making those choices.

You can help them draw on prior knowledge by asking questions or making statements about the materials they have selected: "That mud ball is very large and heavy. How did you change the way you made the raft so that you could keep it afloat?" or "Did you make the raft the same way as you did for that little one?" Observe how the children interact with materials. What choices do you see them making? Look for evidence that children understand the materials. How do you see them using prior knowledge to inform their choices about materials?

This boy has worked hard to construct a raft.

DON'T GET STUCK ON THE "STEPS"

As mentioned earlier, young children engage in the engineering design process constantly, and only occasionally do they do it in a sequenced, ordered way. For that reason, I caution educators against imposing a prescribed set of steps when wishing to provide engineering opportunities. It can be very frustrating for children to be expected to progress through the steps in a linear way. Instead, try to observe how they move in and out of the different phases at different times as their needs require.

During the designing phase, children use their powers of observation to notice that there is a need for something, such as a solution to a problem or an enhancement. For example, several children are working in the sand area to make a castle with a moat. They try to make a bridge out of sand so that their toy horses can get across the moat, but it keeps collapsing. After several attempts to create a bridge out of sand, they discuss their observations of the problem:

> NICO: It needs to be stronger!
>
> CHRISTOPHER: The horses are too heavy!
>
> MIRA: It's not long enough!
>
> FAITH: It's not big enough for the horses. It needs to be sturdier.

Their discussion goes on for a few minutes, during which the children all agree that the bridge itself needs to be stronger to keep from crumbling and to allow the horses to stand on it.

Each child considers possible solutions to the problem. Drawing on his or her prior experience with the materials at hand, and his or her understanding of the properties of those materials, each child starts to think about possible solutions. Soon the children are discussing their solutions:

> MIRA: We got to get some pinecones or something to stack up there in the river [moat].
>
> CHRISTOPHER: We need a branch, like a log or a stick to lay over it like a bridge.
>
> FAITH: A flat branch! A piece of bark!

In this discussion, the children are collaborating to plan their solution. They are hearing one another's ideas and applying those ideas to their own understanding of what's going on. As they discuss their ideas, they work and talk together to plan their solution.

Before long, each child scrambles off to select materials for the bridge. Mira is the first to return, and she stacks the pinecones up in the moat, but they keep falling over and don't provide enough stability for the toy horses to stand on. After a few attempts, she becomes frustrated.

> MIRA: The pinecones won't work . . . they don't hold up the horses and the horses keep falling.
>
> CHRISTOPHER steps in: You need a long, flat branch like this piece of bark.

He removes a few of the pinecones and lays the strip of bark across the sand, spanning the moat. The other children appraise the work, and Mira carefully places two toy horses on the bark. They stay standing, and the children are satisfied with their creation. They quickly resume their imaginary play with the horses.

During this phase of the process, the children have rapidly gone through the create, test, and improve steps. Their first attempt at creating a bridge (Mira's use of pinecones) failed because it did not solve the problem they had originally identified: something was needed to hold the horses up. Placing the horses on the bridge was the "test" cycle. When the test was unsuccessful, they quickly redesigned and improved the solution, using new materials (the strip of bark) and tested it again by placing the horses on the bridge.

While teasing apart the process in which these children engaged helps you to better understand the nuances and stages of the engineering design process, it's important to remember that the progression of thinking, planning, designing, testing, and redesigning is seldom linear for young children. Often children engage in the steps simultaneously, randomly—skipping one or more steps or experiencing them out of sequence (VanMeeteren and Zan 2010). For this reason, educators familiar with young children's development caution against expecting children to progress through every step or to progress through the steps in a particular order each time they are engaged in an engineering investigation. Educators should not expect the sequence of steps to appear linear either; rather, they should note when children are engaged in different steps and how children demonstrate which step they are in.

Math

Perhaps the only domain that gets less love from early childhood educators than science is math. How many people have said at one time or another, "I'm not a math person" or "I don't have the math gene"? It's a sad truth that many early educators tend to avoid math. And if you are one of them, you are not alone! A reported 30 percent of Americans have stated that they would rather clean the bathroom than do a math problem! (Change the equation 2016). In early

This boy is simultaneously testing and redesigning a system he has created for moving logs.

childhood, comfort with math and fluency with the subject can be stronger predictors of later academic success than even literacy. Studies show that children who enter kindergarten with a certain comfort with math go on to be high achievers through their middle and high school years (Claessens and Engel 2013). Researchers have observed children at play and noted that mathematical thinking shows up frequently in play settings (Ginsburg 2006). For example, children's play involves pattern and shapes, comparisons, and numbers. This tells us that young children have an innate curiosity about math and a natural tendency to "think math." As

educators, our job is to help support that curiosity through experience and opportunities for them to engage in math learning and playing. Young children are naturally driven to make sense of things, create representations of things, and solve simple mathematical problems. If asked, they can usually reason and explain their mathematical activities.

Many educators see young children engaging in mathematical play regularly but don't always know how to recognize it or describe specifically what mathematical play looks like. Mathematical play can be play that involves rhythm and patterns, such as songs and dancing, both of which involve an awareness of patterns, rhythm, and spatial sense, such as location, position, direction, and movement. Mathematical play can also include creating things with loose parts, such as pinecones, small stones, or sticks. Children's designs often include symmetry, balance, and repeated patterns. When children engage in dramatic play, such as sharing "cookies" on the playground, playing store, or passing out pretend snacks to their dolls or other toys, they are engaging in math play by subtracting, adding, noting one-to-one correspondence, and practicing representation (using one object to represent another, as when they use small wood chips to represent "money" at the "store").

Large movements, such as climbing, running, and jumping, help children develop their *spatial orientation*. Spatial orientation and awareness are necessary and fundamental math skills that can be practiced often through play (NRC 2009).

IMPORTANT MATH PRACTICES

Just as there are standards, goals, and specific practices related to science and engineering, there are practices associated with math proficiency in young children. Representing, problem solving, reasoning, connecting, and communicating are the process skills important for math proficiency beginning in early childhood (NRC 2009). Sometimes educators refer to the use of these practices as "mathematizing," or viewing a problem or situation through a "math lens."

Many children create patterns, symmetry, and order with materials—several ways that math shows up in their play.

Representing refers to children's ability to represent numbers through written numerals or groups of objects. Problem solving is applying one's experience and understanding to situations to reach a solution. Mathematical reasoning refers to a subset of skills and practices that help children "look beyond surface features of procedures and concepts and see diverse aspects of knowledge as having the same underlying structure" (Baroody, Feil, and Johnson 2007). In other words, reasoning means making sense of the concept of a unit, understanding the number of objects in a group, and recognizing that shapes can be made up of other shapes and that they can be broken down into still others. Reasoning also includes relating and ordering, that is, understanding which is more and which is less in a variety of contexts, such as number, length, and area. It also includes looking for patterns and order, and finally, organizing information.

Children display the ability to make connections in mathematics when they are able to group numbers or create repeating patterns, which forms the basis for multiplication and division. Making connections also includes the ability to describe how things are related in a group or set. In early STEM learning, children frequently play and engage in the world of numbers, geometry, and measurement. Children use numbers in nature play for counting and for representing a number of objects in a set. They engage in measuring when they estimate distances, sizes, and shapes, and even when they look for ways to describe things.

To encourage children to communicate about math, ask them about their thinking. Encourage them to describe to you their understanding of patterns, relationships, similarities, and differences. Ask them about the process they used to make decisions, to sort, to make choices about materials. Listen for them to use mathematical terms, such as *pattern*, *alike/different*, *more than/less than*, and *taller/shorter/higher/deeper*. Look for evidence that they have a sense of cardinaliity (that the last number counted in a set represents the total number of objects), notice the different ways they sort and organize objects and materials. These are fundamental mathematical thinking skills. Their use of mathematical language helps them to be specific about their thinking.

NATURE-BASED MATH TOOLS

Loose parts, described in chapter 2, can be wonderful math tools. They can be sorted, organized, arranged in patterns, used as measuring tools, and more. Children naturally tend to seriate (line up by size) loose parts or use them for measuring (for example, using a stick to measure how deep a puddle is). They organize loose parts such as stones into sets based on measurable attributes such as color or "smooth ones" and " bumpy ones." As you observe children playing and using loose parts, you can ask them about how they are grouping the parts. Use questions such as "How are all of those stones alike?" or "How are those different from these?" These questions encourage them to go deeper and may invite them to sort into new groups. You can encourage children in many ways to identify attributes or characteristics of loose parts. The act of sorting and grouping helps children compare, contrast, and organize.

Developmentally, one of the first things children understand when it comes to math is number and operations. Have you ever heard a child exclaim at snacktime, "She has more than me"? Children have an innate sense that math and quantity matter. And that innate sense is a perfect motivator for learning. Number sense includes counting, one-to-one correspondence, and adding. It includes knowing and understanding how numbers function and how they are relevant in the real world. When children sort and distribute items such as pinecones or shells to their friends during a "picnic" under the trees and they give out one item per child, they are demonstrating a basic awareness of one-to-one correspondence.

Asking children to estimate, visualize, and make predictions about quantity helps them think and communicate mathematically: "Do you think we will find enough berries to fill the bucket? How many handfuls are we going to need?" Adding a question like "Where can we find them?" encourages children to create mental maps of familiar spaces.

Children are also interested in shapes and spatial sense, measurement, and patterns. Loose parts are wonderful for making patterns and can be used in infinite ways. When children design with loose parts, they often naturally try to create symmetry and balance in their creations. They also use loose parts to create shapes, designs, and patterns.

This tendency indicates the beginning of algebraic thinking, as patterns are at the heart of algebra. Identifying shapes and describing spatial relationships are processes at the core of geometry. While most early childhood classrooms are filled with colorful, perfectly shaped cutouts of triangles, squares, and circles, there is more irregularity in the natural world. But geometry is about much more than naming shapes. According to the National Council of Teachers of Mathematics, "The understanding of foundational concepts in three areas of geometry—two- and three-dimensional shapes, spatial relationships, and symmetry and transformations—should be a focus of curriculum experiences for young children" (2000, 96). For that reason, I encourage educators to provide nature-based materials for children to play with these concepts so they can build knowledge and experience. When children play with loose parts, they naturally explore two and three dimensionality, spatial relationships, and symmetry. *Transformation*, in this context, describes the process of flipping, rotating, turning, or otherwise changing the position of something.

Nature provides a lot of math materials!

Stones of various sizes, colors, and textures are useful for a variety of mathematical investigations.

Natural materials and nature-based settings, with their unending variety and diversity, offer children a lot of ways to investigate shapes, spatial relationships, and symmetry. They also embody a variety of attributes. In mathematics, *attribute* is a characteristic used to describe an object. The attribute usually describes the object's shape, size, or color—something that can be measured; for example, the "big, red ball" is a description of an object that is identified by its attributes: its size, color, and shape. You can help children develop their understanding of attributes by asking questions that encourage them to measure, count, compare, and contrast: "**How many** legs does the grasshopper have?"; "**What's the pattern you see** on this caterpillar?"; "**Can you tell me what's**

alike and what's different about these things?"; or, if they choose certain materials in favor of others, "What's different about these things?" or "How are they alike?"

By attending to attributes, children are also engaging in a form of measuring ("This rock has four spots; this rock has two spots . . .") because they are quantifying, or identifying measurable attributes and comparing objects by using these attributes. They are also comparing objects in search of similarities and differences. While most early education classrooms include many objects with clearly defined attributes (such as pattern blocks), natural materials are especially well suited to this purpose because they require young children to identify variations in attributes and thus to be more thoughtful about how certain objects or groups of objects may be alike or different. They require young children to identify and attend to the attributes that matter to them, to create their own systems for sorting and organizing. Also, because of their endless variation, natural materials can be sorted and organized again and again in a variety of ways. For example, Children may sort leaves based on color, then on size, then on shape, texture, or other attributes that they identify.

USE MATH VOCABULARY WHEN POSSIBLE

In early childhood classrooms, teachers often pay particular attention to descriptions or names of shapes. They point out shapes and sizes. But there are many other ways that teachers can engage children in thinking mathematically. Using the appropriate vocabulary in context will help children build their understanding of key math concepts. It's important to use math language when possible, not only for descriptions of things (this is *the edge* of the sidewalk; there is *the side* of that birdhouse), but also in describing what children themselves are doing. Games involving naming shapes, "doing the calendar," and having children help take attendance are common ways that early childhood teachers engage children in math. Those who want to deepen understanding and comfort with math even more can use mathematical terms such as *edge*, *side*, *face*, *corner*, *length*, or *curve* to help children understand how to describe shapes.

Teachers can also use prepositions—terms such as *in*, *on*, *under*, *down*, *next to*, *between*, *beside*, *in back of*, *behind*, *above*, *below*, and *in front of*—to help increase children's spatial awareness and familiarity with the language of math.

In addition to helping you better understand the individual disciplines of STEM, this chapter has presented examples of the thinking practices associated with each discipline and how much they overlap with one another at times. It is because of this overlap that the disciplines of science, technology, engineering, and math complement each other so well in learning and play. There are commonalities in the way that children practice and engage with each of the disciplines and many interconnected ideas. When you can identify and recognize children's tendency to demonstrate the practices in their nature play, you can help deepen their learning in STEM.

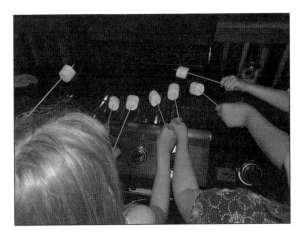

Children's innate understanding of one-to-one correspondence is clear at snacktime!

Building on a Strong STEM Foundation

YOUNG ENGINEERS SOON REALIZE they need a strong foundation in order for their buildings and structures to be tall and wide. With a firm foundation in STEM practices and an eye toward children's natural tendencies to engage in STEM thinking, you can extend your practice even further. This chapter provides a broad overview of some additional approaches to teaching and integrating STEM with young children. Beyond understanding the basic thinking skills associated with STEM, there are additional things that will help you deepen children's learning in STEM disciplines as well as increase your own comfort with STEM and your fluency in recognizing children's natural tendencies to demonstrate STEM practices. Understanding the process of scientific inquiry, knowing the difference between inference and observation, and discerning how to set reasonable outcomes, as well as recognizing the value of discourse and language in children's STEM learning are all key to supporting children's learning and development well.

Children naturally tend to engage in STEM thinking while exploring nature.

The Process of Inquiry

Many educators familiar with science teaching have heard the term *scientific inquiry*, which describes the process of "doing science"—making observations, asking questions, and investigating those questions. Inquiry has become a well-regarded approach for teachers who wish to create more student-centered cultures in their classroom and support children's innate tendency to ask questions and look for answers. It helps children take ownership of their learning, formulate clear questions, and even develop their own investigations. It also has the potential to help children develop their use of the practices described in chapter 3. But inquiry can take many forms, and approaches to inquiry vary depending on a teacher's desired outcomes, the group dynamics, and other factors. The inquiry process is similar to the practices of science described in chapter 3, but there are some differences.

One way to think about inquiry is to view it as a learner-centered approach. In inquiry-based learning, there is a lot of variation in how much control the learner has over the investigation or question, the process of investigating, and the result of the investigation. Many teachers use an inquiry approach when they present children with experiences or phenomena that give rise to rich, investigable questions (questions that can be investigated further). When children are inspired and curious, as they tend to be when the questions are their own, they are more likely to engage more deeply in investigating and learning. As they develop and refine their abilities and comfort with the science practices, they can take more ownership of their learning, determining not just the questions they want to investigate, but how they will do the investigation itself.

This table illustrates that there are a variety of ways to engage learners in the process of inquiry.

	Who has control of the question?	Who determines the materials and procedure?	Who determines the result of the investigation?
Teacher–guided inquiry	Teacher	Teacher	Teacher
	Teacher	Teacher	Student
	Teacher	Student	Student
Student–directed inquiry	Student	Student	Student

This chart draws on ideas from Alan Colburn (1997), M.D. Herron (1971), and Joseph J. Schwab (1962).

As a teacher (particularly if you work with children in the primary grades), you can probably think of times when it's more important to present the specific investigations or specific subjects or questions you want the students in your class to know, rather than having them select the topics or phenomena to be investigated. This is especially true if you are new to STEM investigations, project work, or just not totally sure of your facilitation skills with regard to STEM. Maybe you aren't yet sure how best to support children's investigations and questions, so you want to ease into this a little bit. Also, there have likely been times, or there will be soon, when you have wanted your students to get practice in learning specific STEM practices, such as how to design and conduct investigations or how to respond to an engineering challenge. In these cases, it makes more

You can follow children's interests and also help guide the shape, duration, and focus of their investigations. These children express curiosity about shape, color, buoyancy, and vegetables. They are also investigating how many objects will fit in the bucket and wondering what will happen to these vegetable scraps over time. There is an abundance of rich material for investigation!

sense to allow them the freedom to explore the process of investigating while you concentrate on helping to deepen their work with the practices.

As you become more comfortable with noticing and supporting students' use of the STEM practices, you will find that you become more comfortable with different levels of inquiry as well. Your goals, your program, the amount and quality of resources you have (time, materials, access to natural areas), and the children's interests will all help to determine how deeply and how often to engage in inquiry with your students.

Consider this example: In a typical early childhood setting, the teacher presents the day's activity along with a specific learning objective, which has most likely been identified well in advance. Perhaps it's October and this particular program always has a harvest theme during the month. In this case, the teacher has the most control of the learning. She has identified the objective or questions for investigation (the topic: harvest), the process by which her students will explore that question (the activity she has developed and used for years), and even the answers or resolutions they will determine. For example, a very typical activity for the harvest theme is to estimate how much a pumpkin weighs. The teacher knows how to present this investigation, she has determined what tools to make available for the children's investigation, and she likely knows the answer. This is a very structured investigation. It can be interesting and exciting for children, and it may be their first introduction to use of a scale or the units of measurement used. For some children it may even be their first exposure to a real pumpkin. For the teacher, there are clear benefits as well. Having done this many times before, she knows what to expect of the children, has planned out how she will manage the activity and equipment and how much time to spend before the children lose interest, and even knows what questions the children are likely to ask, so she can prepare ahead of time to make sure she is comfortable with her content knowledge. Finally, she also can assess children's learning because she knows what she wants them to learn.

Another example is a slightly more open-ended activity with which many early childhood educators have some familiarity. Have you ever filled a set of clear sandwich bags with dirt, placed a seed or bean inside, and taped some of the bags to a window and others to a wall that gets no sunlight? The idea behind this investigation is usually to compare the effects of light on the growth of the plant. This is a very teacher-directed inquiry experience. The teacher (or the science kit) has identified the question under investigation and the process by which that question will be investigated, and the teacher already knows the answer.

The value of an activity like this is that it can help children recognize experimental variables (the amount of light the seedling receives) and probably learn about data collection methods and other nuances of conducting guided investigations. In some cases, a little choice is given to children if they are invited to select the location of their experiment (where to tape the baggie). Depending on their age, children may create different graphic organizers for recording their data. They may get some mathematics practice by measuring things like the growth of the plant or hours of sun exposure. These skills are important in the practice of both science and math, so there is nothing wrong with an investigation like this, provided the teacher is clear about its benefits and she is able to focus her attention on supporting the development of those particular skills. As outlined above, there are clear benefits to the teacher as well.

An inquiry investigation that is more student directed might look something like this: After spending time in their school yard and tending their class garden, students may have observed that some plants seem to be taller and stronger than other plants of the same type in the same garden

> Instead of focusing on supporting children's practice with the investigation process itself, a common pitfall with an experiment such as this one is that the teacher may focus on the success of growing bean plants, thereby shifting the focus entirely away from the practices of identifying a research question, conducting an investigation and collecting data. Focusing on the success of the plants also sets some children up to feel as though they have somehow failed if their plants don't grow as expected. A great deal of learning in science and engineering happens when things don't go as planned, and that could be a missed opportunity. When that happens, teacher and children lose the opportunity to develop the STEM process skills that are at the heart of this type of activity.

bed. They express their curiosity about why plants grow better in one section of the garden bed than another. The teacher helps them clarify their question into one that can be investigated, and then he provides materials that they can use to investigate their question together. While the teacher has provided an assortment of different materials, the children decide together how to use them and which ones will work best to conduct their investigations. This example shows what student-directed inquiry looks like.

Planting a seed in a plastic bag and affixing it to the window is an experience with a structured science investigation. There are many ways to make science investigations more open-ended.

In early childhood education settings, as well as settings where the teacher or children may not have had a lot of practice creating their own investigations, totally student-directed inquiry can be very challenging to manage. This is largely because there are so many variables, including the strength of the question (how easily children can investigate it with the tools and materials they have available); their comfort and experience with the tools and materials available; the amount of time involved; their ability to self-direct and the role and responsibilities of the teacher.

For this reason, it is often better to scaffold your own experiences with inquiry as you and your students become more familiar with all of those variables. Many teachers move across the spectrum of inquiry, affording their students more or less freedom depending on the circumstances. You can introduce this level of freedom gradually so that your students are familiar with the tools available, the process of identifying and investigating questions, and, of course, the STEM habits of mind that will enable them to be successful.

BUT WHAT ABOUT CONTENT?

At times, of course, a teacher wants her students to learn specific content. For example, a teacher who has a learning outcome for her class that students will understand that some seeds travel on air may craft an experience that leads the students to that particular piece of content *as well as* provides a lot of hands-on experience and engagement. She might start by asking the children, "How do seeds travel?" and then provide them with opportunities to investigate different types of seeds and learn about how they travel—through the air, by clinging to fabric or fur, or by rolling or being moved, for example. By introducing an investigation with a question, the teacher helps guide students' attention to particular content elements she wants them to be aware of, and this helps them to be selective about the details on which they choose to focus.

The question "How do seeds travel?" identifies a specific content target for children (that seeds move from place to place; some seeds travel on air, some fall to the ground, and others are transported by clinging to surfaces such as fabric and fur). The teacher-provided question helps narrow children's focus as they explore. Instead of noticing a large quantity of details about all kinds of seeds, the teacher's question helps the children focus their attention: they pay particular attention to information that helps them develop answers to that question. They may look at where acorns fall to the ground, they may recall times when they have had cockleburs or other seeds stuck to their socks after a hike, and they may think and talk about what kinds of seeds they have seen traveling on air (such as dandelion seeds or samaras—commonly known as "helicopters"). They may notice that air-traveling seeds tend to have some things in common, and they may speculate about how the shape, size, and structure of seeds makes a difference in how they travel. To support their learning this content, the teacher would spend time with the children handling, comparing, identifying and describing the shapes, sizes, and structures of each seed (its attributes). Perhaps she would provide ways for children to represent the seeds, such as through drawing or clay sculpture.

Same Activity, Different Goals

If the teacher's goal was instead to provide the students with experience using tools and technology to investigate scientific phenomena, she might provide hand lenses, thin nets, or other tools for the children to catch, carry, and explore seeds. They would learn, through firsthand experience, that some tools work well for capturing certain kinds of seeds and others don't work as well. They would learn how to physically manipulate the tools, such as hand lenses, magnifying boxes, nets, and whatever else the teacher provides. Once the children have had plenty of hands-on time with seeds and the tools for collecting them, depending on their age, she might encourage them to collect video or still images of the seeds with digital cameras, which the class could review and discuss at a later time. This is a valuable experience with using tools and technology in the service of learning.

Maybe this teacher wants her students, instead, to gain practice creating questions that can be investigated. In STEM these are known as "investigable" questions. The teacher would likely spend a good deal of time outdoors, allowing her students to gain plenty of firsthand experience with seeds and trees. She would want them to experience seeds in all seasons and all kinds of weather so that they would have a lot of material to inform their thinking. Next, she might start a list titled "What are all of the things we wonder about seeds and trees?" and invite all kinds of ideas, comments, and thoughts about seeds and trees. From that list, she could identify the statements that are investigable and help the children investigate. For example, "Does every tree in the school yard produce seeds?" is a question that can be investigated, but "Do trees like to make seeds?" is not. One way to determine whether a question can be investigated is to look at a statement and ask yourself, "Can I find out more using the available time and materials?" If the answer is yes, move forward. If the answer is no, set aside the question and select another.

This child is investigating "How far down does the sand go?"

Observation and Inference

Observation and inference are two practices in STEM thinking that are especially important because they help students develop fluency in the fundamental skills that lead to investigations. Observing is the art of noticing details, and it is an important STEM skill that is central to developing fluency in science and mathematics practices. To practice observation, one needs to look closely, to watch or monitor an object or event for some time in order to notice details and other significant elements. Observation also happens when one looks closely at something, studying the fine details. Observation can be practiced by taking time to quietly focus on something, or it can happen in the hustle and bustle of a busy day. Teachers can help children refine their skills of observation by providing plenty of opportunities for them to observe things. Very young children can be encouraged to observe by sitting quietly outdoors or describing the things they see, hear, and feel. Teachers may encourage older children to write or draw their observations, represent them with clay or other materials, or note them by labeling parts of an illustration. Discussing children's observations is also very important, so be sure to allow numerous opportunities for children to share their observations with one another and with you.

There are many ways to engage children in observation through nature experiences; indeed, because there are so many details to observe, it is the best environment in which to practice observation. Children engaged in observation are naturally inclined to consider what elements or details are important to attend to. For example, if someone wants to draw or create a representation of a special rock, he will need to consider which details are important for that representation. Is the color important? The texture? The shape of the rock? If he needed to describe the rock to a friend so that she could find it among a collection of similar rocks, he may select different or additional details to attend to, such as distinctive features like chips or rounded edges.

STEM Start

Children can look closely at tree bark and notice the number of colors or shapes present in the bark. They can look at leaves and count the points or lobes as part of their observation. (Bonus: This also helps them identify and count measurable attributes, an important math skill.)

Observation can be practiced anywhere outdoors. One of the wonderful things about nature is that it provides opportunities to observe sweeping landscapes and floating clouds, as well as tiny details like wrinkled bark or the antennae of a grasshopper. Children enjoy opportunities to look closely at the shapes, sizes, and details found in nature, and they will find no shortage of interesting things to observe.

STEM Start

Another way to practice the skill of observation is to place a few like natural objects, such as a few pinecones, in an opaque fabric bag or other container. Have children reach in and try to describe the objects they are feeling. The goal is *not* to name the object but to notice details and make observations about what they feel. It can be very challenging, especially for younger children, not to call out, "Pinecones!" as soon as they identify the object. Help them develop self-regulation by encouraging them to share their ideas about what the objects feel like instead of calling out the names of the objects. Encourage them to use words such as *cool* or *warm*, *hard* or *soft*, *bumpy* or *smooth*. This can be a fun and engaging game for children of all ages, and older children can be challenged not to repeat another word someone else has already used. You can also give them all their own "mystery bag" and invite them to draw the object inside just by gathering information about its size, shape, and texture through feeling the object. This is great for older children and provides an opportunity to use spatial thinking skills by rotating and visualizing the object and then representing it as a two-dimensional drawing.

Observations can be made with every sense. While young children will have different levels of sensory acuity (that is, some will have a stronger sense of smell than others, or a greater sensitivity to texture or sound), they all enjoy using a variety of senses to make observations about the natural world. And there are plenty of things to smell, feel, see, hear, and even taste in nature!

Listening observations often include birdsongs, traffic noises, and other familiar outdoor sounds. Often children find that they can hear well when their eyes are closed. Many educators like this activity because it is another opportunity to practice self-regulation, since it encourages children to quiet their bodies and their minds. We make observations constantly, and slowing down and paying close attention to those observations can be useful.

The habit of inference is often confused with observation. The two skills are often used together, but they aren't interchangeable. The process of inferring means attaching meaning to something based on the observations you have made. It is what leads a young child to shout out, "Pinecones!" when he feels them in the pillowcase in the example above, rather than simply describing them. (To make that game one of inference, then, you could encourage the child to name the object.)

For another example of inference, imagine you are in a quiet forest at the water's edge and you suddenly hear a dog bark, the crashing of something moving through the underbrush, and then see a flock of ducks fly overhead. In this setting, you might infer that a dog was chasing the ducks and scared them away. Your observations were what you heard and identified through sound and sight. Your inference was the conclusion that you made based on what you observed.

STEM Start

Sit together in a circle outdoors. Have the children listen for sounds and hold up one finger for each sound they hear. While counting is an important skill in and of itself, this becomes a nice exercise in spatial awareness when children are also challenged to point in the direction from where the sounds originate.

Understanding the difference between observation and inference is essential, because in STEM these are each distinct steps that lead to meaning-making. We make observations and inferences all the time, and practicing both skills is necessary, as well as knowing the difference between the two. Here is a way to distinguish between observation and inference.

What do you see in the three frames below? What story does it tell?

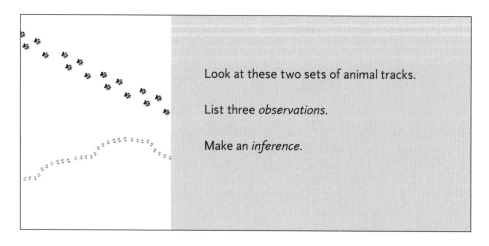

Look at these two sets of animal tracks.

List three *observations*.

Make an *inference*.

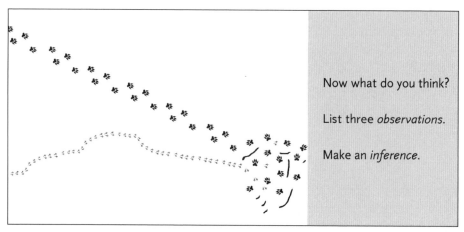

Now what do you think?

List three *observations*.

Make an *inference*.

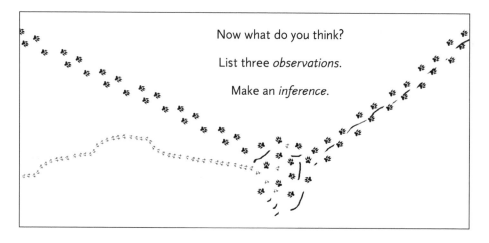

Now what do you think?

List three *observations*.

Make an *inference*.

Inferences can be particularly powerful when they arise as a result of discourse. When children engage in STEM investigations together with their teacher, they often share ideas based on their observations and use one another's prior knowledge to help them make inferences together, leading to a shared understanding of phenomena. When children engage in collaborative work to sort out their observations, they often help one another make meaning from those observations.

THE IMPORTANCE OF LANGUAGE AND DISCOURSE

As educators who focus on literacy have long understood, introducing words in context is the most effective way to help children learn new vocabulary. This is also the case when it comes to STEM, particularly in science and mathematics. When children investigate scientific phenomena and then have the chance to process that experience through reflection and discussion with one another and their teachers using scientifically informed language, they are more likely to build the content knowledge that is so important later on. Scientifically informed language (or academic language) is language that describes phenomena or any objects and processes with which children engage. You can hear examples of this type of language when children use words that describe the properties of materials, when they describe things using mathematical language (as described in chapter 3), when they are able to articulate how they engaged in the design process, or when they describe the functions of technology or machines with appropriate vocabulary. Use of academic language in context fosters literacy and language development. In addition to supporting individual learning, language also helps groups construct knowledge together through discussion and discourse.

These children discuss their discoveries together and share ideas.

In the scientific community, discourse is a type of dialogue; it's a conversation about ideas. It's the conversation that happens when individuals share insights, ask questions of one another, explain their points of view, and build off one another's thinking to make meaning. Discourse is how children explore, explain, and develop their ideas in groups. Creating a community of discourse is important for any class because it has great power to help children clarify their thinking together in response to new experiences.

One way that some teachers encourage discourse is to facilitate "science talks" after children have had experiences with new phenomena or materials.

These children are helping to build a campfire and discussing the process and their observations.

During these talks, children share their thinking and reflect on their questions and experience among their peers. They can discuss math as well, sharing problem-solving strategies and reviewing their own thinking about how they used math. These strategies and practices help children build understanding. Children share ideas and explore their thinking together. Teachers encourage the free flow of ideas, listening for understanding. Rather than correcting misconceptions or lecturing about content, teachers listen to the children's ideas, repeating them back or asking probing questions to help children shape their understanding. When misconceptions do emerge, teachers use it as an opportunity to examine children's thinking and provoke further investigation. With math and engineering learning, discourse allows children and teachers to reflect on their thinking and their approaches to solving problems, and it provides a space for the class community to process errors together. Explaining to children that "this is how scientists make meaning" or "this is how we explore our science ideas" can help to build their sense of confidence in sharing their questions and ideas. It also fosters a sense of community within the class where it is okay not to know all the answers. We rely on our peers to help us understand. Discourse is important because it helps children think through and describe their observations. It helps them construct explanations and make predictions based on experience. Ultimately, when science talks or math talks become a routine part of the day, children's sense of self-efficacy can be supported as well, and the conversations become rich, collaborative opportunities for children to construct knowledge together as a community.

Like adults, children need opportunities to talk about and explain their reasoning, ask questions of one another, and discuss their ideas among a community of peers. A classroom environment that is safe, nonjudgmental, and welcoming of ideas supports children's learning and development in STEM and many other areas. Like adults, children develop understanding by expressing their ideas, challenging one another's ideas and conclusions (respectfully), and creating meaning through discourse. In expressing their ideas about phenomena, problems, or ideas, children engage in the mental process of reflecting on their own thinking, clarifying their ideas, and expressing them in ways that their peers can understand and respond to. This is a fundamental part of how children experience learning in STEM and how they develop the ideas and practices that will further their understanding. Educators who value and make time for classroom discourse attest to the importance of community in the development of ideas—the meaning-making that is so important in science and other disciplines.

What does discourse look like in the classroom? Often, discourse happens during shared snacktime or lunchtime. A child may remark on something that happened outside that she found particularly interesting. Another child will respond with her thoughts, and the teacher may ask clarifying questions, repeating the children's ideas and helping to draw out more information about the children's thinking by encouraging them

These boys are sharing their ideas about what makes their boats float so well.

to continue sharing their ideas. She may ask other children, "Sonja thought the worm didn't like it when she shined the flashlight on it because it started to squirm away. Did anyone else see that? Joey, what do you think that worm was doing?" This type of engagement helps the children reflect on their own experience and their own thinking. This is not the time to correct any "wrong ideas." It's the time to listen respectfully to one another, to ask the children for clarification so you can get a sense of what they know. If you continually hear children talking about a shared misconception, use that as evidence that you need to spend some more time with that phenomena. Provide more time and experience to help them construct more knowledge. You might present new information or provide new tools to help them investigate the phenomena more deeply, which might help to correct their misconceptions.

Discourse also supports the development of additional soft skills critically important in STEM learning, such as curiosity (about one another's ideas, procedures, and experiences), respect for evidence (learning about sound reasoning and connecting it to why things created certain results, or "how I know"), and flexibility (the ability to change or adapt one's thinking based on new information or ideas).

STEM education is an opportunity to provide children with opportunities to investigate, explore, make meaning, and communicate their ideas. When your actions, questions, discussions, and classroom activities support those investigations, you are providing children with opportunities not only to deepen their experience with these practices but also to construct knowledge through first-hand experience and inquiry.

Consider Your Outcomes and the Children's Needs

Young children have very different needs when it comes to STEM in the classroom. And your needs are different as well. For example, you may have teaching outcomes that involve particular STEM concepts or practices, or they may involve content, or they may be focused more on helping children become more familiar with using specific tools and technology. The learning outcomes you set for your students will affect how you craft and conduct your outdoor investigations.

Often, out of a desire to show children something exciting and novel, teachers work hard to raise funds and organize enriching field trips to zoos, nature centers, or other compelling outdoor environments. Outdoor-based field trips can connect a school's or district's curricular material to the outdoor setting, and they provide children (and adults!) with opportunities to explore natural areas that they may not otherwise have access to. While field trips are often exciting and memorable, without a concerted effort on the part of the teacher to integrate the learning material "after the fact," they seldom have a lasting impact on young children's understanding of science (Biggs and Tap 1986). This may be due to the novelty, relatively short duration of time, and unfamiliar surroundings presented by most field trip excursions.

On the other hand, when children in preschool, kindergarten, and the primary grades are given the opportunity to engage *frequently and consistently* with *familiar* natural settings, their learning is deeper and richer (ibid.). They are better able to generalize the learning that occurs in these natural settings outdoors. Perhaps this is because when they have access to a natural setting on a regular basis, they can make continuous observations over time, leading to a richer understanding of phenomena, such as seasonal changes, weather, life cycles, interactions between and among insects and animals, plants and plant communities, and systems such as the water cycle. All of these observations connect directly to the disciplines of STEM and offer potential for deep investigation. Also, the knowledge and familiarity that children develop with repeated visits to a natural area can lead to a greater sense of stewardship and responsibility for the natural world (Wells and Lekies 2006).

In early childhood, children are most engaged with the familiar, so outcomes and objectives that involve familiar surroundings (for example, caring for the school yard, identifying plants and animals that live there, counting species, matching and exploring colors, exploring size and distances, counting steps from the tree to the classroom door) will be very meaningful. Young children are very concerned with what is tangible and immediate, so setting outcomes that engage them in the process of caring for, experiencing, and exploring tangible, available things will be fulfilling and meaningful.

Experiences that respond to children's natural self-centeredness are also appropriate for early childhood. Children are interested in how things directly impact them as well as how they can directly impact things. Teachers who strive for nature-based STEM learning are often eager to teach children about environmental issues so that they will be more likely to demonstrate responsibility and environmental stewardship. In early childhood, however, joy and delight in the natural world should be the primary goal of an educator when it comes to nature-based learning. Helping children find joy in discovery and investigation will help them become lifelong learners, driven by curiosity. Young children need time to have authentic, joyful experiences with nature in all its forms and all its contexts so that they are free to develop a deep, abiding love for nature that will naturally lead to responsibility and stewardship as they grow. Young children are not emotionally prepared to deal with the frightening and overwhelming environmental issues that confront us; there is plenty of time later in their schooling for that. Even if they seem "wise beyond their years" or you are tempted to teach environmental issues out of your own sense of passion, I urge you to hold off. Let them play and delight in nature for a bit longer.

When children engage frequently with a place, it becomes familiar and very special.

Children experience joy and delight in the natural world.

Putting It All Together

By now, I hope you are feeling both pleasantly surprised by how much STEM-related work you and your students are already doing and inspired to do even more. This chapter provides an overview of different strategies that you can employ as you move toward deeper nature-based STEM integration. It also guides you through an assessment of your program, including your outdoor environment, resources that complement your investigations, how you can make your indoor environment more conducive to nature-based investigations, planning for safety, and specific strategies to deepen children's investigations through guided classroom talks, carefully crafted questions, and documentation produced together.

As I mentioned in chapter 2, a growing number of early childhood settings strive for strong connections to the natural world. As with so much else, there is a spectrum. In some cases, this means dedicated time outdoors each day, and in other cases, schools do not go indoors at all—the children nap, snack, and play outdoors all day long. Most care settings fall somewhere between these two points on the spectrum.

Children benefit from time outdoors in all kinds of weather.

As you continue to expand your STEM investigations to include the natural world, you and your colleagues may want to consider how much STEM to focus on and where you can increase the opportunities for children to engage naturally in STEM practices. Whatever approach you take will be a positive step toward increasing nature connections for young children, supporting their natural tendencies to practice STEM, and setting them on a path for success as learners well into the future.

Integrating the STEM Disciplines

Integration is central to high-quality STEM education. When children make connections across disciplines, they are better able to make sense of the material and thus understand how it all comes together in real life. As you have seen, there is a great deal of overlap across the STEM disciplines, and many of the activities and investigations you choose to engage in will lend themselves to learning about each of the areas. Of course, even though STEM engagement comes naturally to children and more intentionally connecting the disciplines may go seamlessly for you, as with anything, it requires careful planning. How do you know where to begin? How much STEM will you strive to include?

Although it may seem counterintuitive, teachers of young children need not design curriculum or plan activities specifically based on the seasons or predetermined themes or units, as is often the case. With nature, there are so many more options, which in many cases are more enriching and meaningful to children than any kit or predetermined theme could be. When children play in nature, they are often engaged in the very practices and habits of science that "boxed" curriculum aims to teach. And nature provides plenty of stimuli and material from which to launch investigations and projects that explore STEM concepts in depth. When you identify children's specific interests, you can help shape experiences that support their learning concepts, practice the skills and processes of math, science, and engineering, and use technology in ways that help them investigate or construct knowledge.

While you may not need a prescribed curriculum, when moving toward a more nature-based context for your STEM education, it is still important to plan ahead. As you consider how you will use the outdoor resources available to you, you will want to ensure you have addressed the details that can potentially impact your and your students' experience. Thinking carefully about the surroundings, resources, opportunities, and challenges that spending time outside presents will pay off in the long run, as you will be better prepared for whatever comes your way.

SAFETY CONCERNS

Some of the most common concerns that arise for early childhood teachers revolve around safety. This is natural and understandable, since caring for children is a big responsibility! Not only do you strive to keep all the children in your care safe from harm, but you also want them to be comfortable, excited and engaged during outdoor STEM investigations. Taking precautions to ensure everyone's safety will help you and the children in your care relax and enjoy the outdoor explorations.

Remember that children with life-threatening allergies (such as to bee stings, tree nuts, peanuts, or eggs) may need extra consideration when exploring outdoors. If you have children with allergies in your care, always carry emergency epinephrine. Note that some birdseed contains nuts, and that nuts and eggshells are sometimes found in garden mulch and even some potting soils. Check labels carefully every time you use these materials, and consult the allergic child's parent or primary care-

Adult supervision is an important factor in keeping children safe, especially at the beginning of a school year or for groups new to unstructured outdoor play.

giver for additional precautions that might be necessary. Birdseed and gardening materials without nuts or eggshells are available, and it's worth seeking them out to ensure the safety of all children. Be sure you are aware of any potential allergens that may be present. Even if you don't have children with a known

allergy in your classroom, many states allow teachers to carry emergency epinephrine—about one out of thirteen children have life-threatening food allergies, so it pays to be prepared. It's worth taking precautions to keep children safe "just in case." An estimated 25 percent of first-time allergic reactions happen in school settings (McIntyre et al. 2005).

Insect Bites and Stings

Teach children how to behave around bees and wasps to avoid being stung. Rather than panicking and waving their arms about, staying still or simply walking away is a good strategy to avoid a bee sting. Of course, sometimes stings still happen regardless

These children get up close and personal with honeybees to learn about their life cycle and role in nature. Learning about bees can help alleviate children's anxieties about them.

STEM Start
As scary as bees and wasps may be for young children, insect encounters present many STEM teaching opportunities. You might notice a child's fear and let that lead to an investigation about the role of these insects in nature, such as for pollinating plants or serving as food sources for other animals. You might take the opportunity to look closely at the insects (if the child is comfortable or willing to give it a try) to learn more about their bodies and the way they work.

of precautions, so carrying a first aid kit that includes emergency epinephrine and ice packs in the event of a sting is always a good idea.

Some parents prefer that their children wear bug repellent when outdoors to avoid mosquito bites and ticks. The Environmental Protection Agency and the Centers for Disease Control assert that there is no known risk to children from the use of DEET-containing insect repellent (see "Insect Repellent Use & Safety" on page 193); however, many parents and teachers have preferences when it comes to preventing insect bites, so be sure you are aware of those preferences.

Weather and Sunburn

Before venturing outdoors, you need to consider whether the children in your program may need additional gear to be warm and comfortable during any kind of weather. Many teachers report that one of the biggest barriers to getting their classes outdoors is the lack of appropriate outerwear. In some climates, winter weather poses a risk of discomfort. In areas that get very cold, it is critical that children have appropriate outerwear to ensure that they are comfortable and

STEM Start
Changing temperatures outdoors present a great opportunity for children to learn about heat loss and insulation. The human body is constantly trying to maintain a regular temperature and gains and loses heat all the time, mostly through the head, hands, and feet (this is why warm socks, mittens, and hats are so important!). We generate body heat mostly through physical activity. Clothing layers such as hats or wool mittens themselves do not "make you warmer"—they keep your body warm by preventing heat loss. Some materials and fabrics are much better at this than others. Can you think of any examples?

warm. Each site will have its own policy for how cold is "too cold" to take children outdoors, but know that there are plenty of forest kindergartens and other outdoor schools that operate in temperatures as low as the single digits and beyond. It takes some getting used to, and proper gear is a must. When children (and teachers!) are dressed appropriately, this is perfectly safe and poses no threat to children's health.

To ensure that all children have appropriate outerwear, here are several possible solutions:

- Proper gear is clearly explained in the parent handbook of many schools that require parents to supply whatever clothing children need to be comfortable. A gear list is sent home at the beginning of the school year, and parents are asked to provide a set of "outdoor shoes" or boots, a change of clothes, rain gear (jacket and pants), a sun hat, and appropriate winter gear for their climate. In some schools, money from a scholarship or other fund is used to provide extra gear for families who can't afford these items.

- Some schools host "swap meets" where families can donate outdoor gear that their children have outgrown and/or trade it for clothing of the proper size. The school administration may keep a basket of extra or leftover clothing from the swap meet to ensure that every child has something appropriate to wear.

- Some schools request that families purchase or donate an extra set of rain gear, mittens, hats, or whatever items they can afford at the beginning of the year.

- Some teachers approach local outdoor and recreational stores for donations or apply for community grants or donations of gear for their students.

Whatever approach you take, the point is to make sure that all children have the gear they need to venture outside often throughout the day and to be comfortable.

Just as children need to be warm and dry during cold weather, they need to be comfortable and safe during hot weather too. Be sure to provide plenty of sunscreen for the children in your care. Many programs request that parents provide, and in some cases apply, sunscreen on their

Appropriate gear for all children ensures that they will be comfortable, safe, and free to enjoy nature no matter what the weather.

own children. The SunWise program, a project of the National Environmental Education Foundation that stresses the importance of sun protection, recommends SPF 50. Note that many sunscreens contain nut-based derivatives or other allergens that can be problematic for some children, so be mindful of any allergies and be aware of parental preferences regarding the use and application of sunscreen. Proper hydration is important too, and some children need to be reminded to drink plenty of water during outdoor excursions to prevent dehydration. As a way of reducing waste through use of disposable bottles, many programs aim to provide children with a reusable water bottle to keep at school. Consider seeking donations from local outdoor stores if resources are an issue.

CLASSROOM EXPECTATIONS

Classroom expectations and norms are an important part of keeping everyone safe as well. One effective and inclusive way to address safety issues is to have children participate in the process of establishing group norms and expectations (mutually agreed upon behaviors to facilitate learning) rather than simply imposing a set of hard-and-fast rules on the children. The work of talking together about safety and expectations for outdoor learning can help build investment in the classroom culture and make it more likely that students will maintain their commitment to those norms. This is especially true at the beginning of the school year when going outdoors may still be regarded as a novelty and children occasionally have trouble remembering that there are expectations about being outdoors, just as there are about class time indoors. Children love—and deserve to be—involved in making rules and establishing the norms of a classroom community.

Catalysts for Learning

In science a catalyst is something that causes a reaction or a chemical change. In STEM education, catalysts can also be things that prompt change in a person's thinking or understanding. What are the catalysts for learning in early childhood? Think about the things that prompt children to become engaged in learning or discovery. Novelty, such as new materials or experiences, is a powerful prompt to engage children in investigations. In most cases, though, you don't need to provide new materials or create new experiences for your students to become engaged in STEM. Sometimes it's just a matter of looking around at the resources available; your existing classroom tools, supplies, and equipment; your classroom space and setting; and of course, the outdoor areas available to you for nature-based learning and play.

MATERIALS AND TOOLS

Resource Inventory

Where do children naturally do STEM outdoors? What places do they gravitate toward? Before answering this question, you may wish to observe children at play for a number of days or weeks. See if you can determine what areas of the school yard hold the most interest for them. Where do they tend to engage with one another for collaborative play? Where do they have access to living things, such as plants? Do they have access to loose parts, such as pinecones, stones, sticks, and sand? What do they like to do with them?

Pay attention to the places and things that children are curious about. These children are investigating a familiar log.

After considering these questions, think about ways that you can intentionally and thoughtfully create opportunities that invite children to go deeper with their natural investigations and questions. Are there additional natural materials that you could provide, such as plants or stones? What tools and technology would help the children explore phenomena and materials to construct knowledge?

Let's consider a typical early childhood school yard. Look for features and elements that will engage children in STEM process skills. How can you expose them to experiences and phenomena that will elucidate science and engineering concepts? How can you provide opportunities for them to use math? What opportunities exist for them to practice using tools and technology to investigate their world?

For many educators, a school yard garden is the most obvious place to introduce STEM opportunities. A garden can be a rich source of opportunities for children to investigate phenomena such as seasonal changes, plant structure and form, earth materials (sand, soil, mud, gravel, and mulch), temperature changes, insects and invertebrates, seeds, foods, and more. The water cycle and plant life cycles can be investigated here too. Remember to listen to and observe the children in your care— their observations and questions will lead to investigations that may deeply engage them in STEM. If your center is located in a very urban area, even the parking lot or sidewalk can present a STEM-rich learning opportunity. You will be surprised by how many opportunities exist for you to investigate.

A garden is a year-round provocation for learning and play. Here a group of children are beginning to get a garden bed ready for planting, while others simply play and investigate in the dirt.

Do you have a post-and-platform play structure? If so, even that can provide some opportunities for STEM investigations. For example, notice how the children experiment with balance and center of gravity as they play on a teeter-totter. A playground slide provides opportunities to experiment with an inclined plane or ramp. And if you are lucky enough to have sand in your play area, you have plenty of opportunities for STEM learning. Sand offers an invitation to dig, pile, tunnel, and push it around. Children love to scoop and carry sand. They can be mesmerized by its softness, its coolness and warmth, and the different sizes of sand grains. Children drag sticks across sand and create patterns and designs, experimenting with aesthetics. They vary the amount of pressure on the stick to create new patterns, and in doing so, they learn about tool use and the properties of sand and other materials, such as sticks, leaves, pine needles, and stones. They dig deep holes and discover the damp layers of sand hidden beneath. They look for opportunities to move it from place to place. Sand on the surface of a slide or platform changes its texture completely, offering new sensory input and varying the physical challenge of walking or moving on that surface.

If you feel that your space simply has "no nature," look very closely. What resources are available? Is there even a single tree that children could get to know? A fence that could be moved to provide more access? Is there a place to set up container gardens? Talk to your colleagues and the parent community. Once they realize the benefits of nature-based play and learning, they will likely be willing to work with you to create opportunities for children to get more experience with nature. Creative efforts such as garden beds and potted plants can provide young children with connections to nature.

Once you have looked at your surroundings, you have probably identified many opportunities for increasing STEM engagement. Here are some recommendations for adding elements to your outdoor play space to support nature-based STEM learning:

- natural surfaces such as grass, gravel, wood chips, or pine needles

- piles of dirt and sand for digging

- an area for mud play

- access to water, such as a hose or hand pump, with plenty of containers nearby, such as scoops, shovels, buckets, bags, ramps, tubes, and sprinkling cans

- varying terrain, such as small hills, valleys, child-sized stepping-stones, and bridges

- trees that bear fruit and flowers, plants and shrubs with beautiful textures and scents

- pathways that children can follow

- places where children can hide, such as willow houses, shrubs, and even sheets or play canopies

- plants and trees with a variety of textures, heights, and shapes

- ramps and tubes for moving things

- loose parts, such as pinecones, stones, sticks, acorns, flowers, leaves, and other interesting items from nature (See appendix B for more suggestions.)

Tall grasses or shrubby areas offer places for children to play, hide, and just be.

SPECIAL NEEDS

If you have children in your program with special needs, consider how you will accommodate them. No outdoor experience is enjoyable if someone from the classroom community is excluded. Craft your experiences and your time outdoors carefully and thoughtfully to include everyone. All of the children in your care should have the opportunity to experience the joyful freedom of outdoor learning. If your site is not ADA accessible, find out what you need to do in order to make it so, or find a place that is accessible to all. Explore assistive equipment, such as ramps or "bumbo" seats, or other ways to create access for children to engage in outdoor activity. Employ platforms or planting tables to hold loose parts so that children in wheelchairs may have access to natural materials as well. Consider how you can modify experiences, equipment, and expectations to ensure that all children can enjoy nature-based learning. Appendix A has resources for you to consider.

Remember that children with sensory issues may not be comfortable touching or playing in the mud, but they may still be very curious about it. Providing plenty of spoons, gloves, and other tools that will allow children to explore the mud without touching it or getting messy will help create an inclusive community. This will provide not only equal access, but a great opportunity to explore the benefits and drawbacks of different types of tools: What kinds of tools allow you to scoop up the most mud without getting any on your hands? What kinds of tools hold mud the best? How can you separate the gravel from the mud?

EATING AND PICKING

While picnics and snacktime outdoors are great for building community, and a fine time to practice discourse and idea sharing—very appropriate activities to do at any time of year—I strongly encourage teachers to establish a "no eating anything the teacher does not provide" rule that applies to your nature explorations. Although some edible plants can be found in even the most urban areas, food allergies and sensitivities, as well as the abundance of pesticides and other chemicals sprayed on landscapes and vegetation, make it particularly important that children be supervised by an adult and never eat anything unless given the okay by a grown-up who is certain that it is safe.

A girl picks a ripe apple from a tree.

One of my earliest memories of learning outdoors was when my class was invited to harvest dandelions to make dandelion fritters! It was a strange experience for me at age seven, but I remember it vividly, from harvesting the dandelions to removing the flowerheads to the scent of cooking oil and cinnamon sugar as we fried them up

If you wish to create opportunities to provide delicious fruits and vegetables for the children in your care to enjoy, find out what gardening zone your site falls within. If you have space and a proper site for planting, you can create an edible landscape that will offer plenty of delicious juicy fruits and vegetables. Numerous resources are available for classroom gardens. See appendix A for suggestions.

A boy looks through a thin, clear piece of ice on a winter day.

COLLECTING, DISPLAYING, AND USING OBJECTS FROM NATURE

The more connection children can have with real objects from nature, the better. Obviously the best place for this to happen is outdoors, but there will no doubt be times when you can't get outside or when children want to bring their treasures inside. Whenever possible, make bringing nature indoors an option. Some teachers set up nature tables or science stations filled with important objects that children have collected. Some teachers rotate the objects; for example, they set out an assortment of beautifully arranged shells one month and stones the next to inspire children's questions. Think through how you will approach the use of natural materials in the classroom. Where will they be located? Throughout the room or in a special area reserved for nature items? How will you let children know it is okay to touch and explore the materials? Will the materials be available for art and dramatic play if children wish to incorporate them into these activities? Consider how you will create space and opportunities for children to use objects during their dramatic play. Items such as "tree cookies" (thin, sanded slices of tree trunks or branches) are favorites, but children also love to use sticks, fresh leaves, gourds, shells, pebbles, dried seed heads, and other natural materials in dramatic play both inside the classroom and out. Make sure the items are accessible and available.

Natural materials can add interesting elements to children's art, and some children love to use them for collages, as tools for painting, and as textural elements in their compositions. Will you make natural materials available for use in art?

Thoughtfully collecting special artifacts, such as shapely sticks, special rocks and shells, or other natural treasures, can enhance a child's connection to nature through providing a tangible connection to their outdoor adventures. You can also bring nature objects back into the classroom to serve as loose parts in play, to help create a sense of reverence for nature, and to inspire questions and a sense of wonder in children. Many natural objects also serve as great tools for scientific investigations.

Natural materials can be used in many ways. This artistic representation of a dragon is made from pine needles, cones, and willow leaves.

Many educators understandably feel that taking "souvenirs" from nature encourages a consumer mentality. Some feel it can negatively impact plant populations, and in some places it does. In some locations, such as national parks and some state parks, collecting *any* objects from nature is illegal. Collecting feathers or any body parts from birds from any site, including private property, is also illegal, as migratory birds are protected under special laws that prohibit collection of nests, eggs, and feathers. As you consider your approach to collecting, be sure that you understand the laws in your state and county, and know whether the land you intend to use for your explorations is private or public property. If you take excursions to nearby parks or nature centers, call ahead and speak with park staff to learn about the rules for each site.

Tools for Documenting Learning

SCIENCE NOTEBOOKS AND JOURNALS

Science notebooks are tools used by educators, often in the upper elementary and middle school grades. They offer students a place to record their ideas, make sketches, write down questions, document procedures of investigations, and synthesize learning. They can also be used with younger children when teachers take special considerations to ensure their use supports joy and wonder in learning.

A science notebook can be a place where older children record data and jot notes about the procedures they follow during their investigations. Children can also use them to make sketches or observational drawings of natural objects

These children are used to the routine of using their science notebooks every day. Here they get ready to reflect on their time in nature.

they encounter, such as rocks, sticks, feathers, or flowers, or to illustrate their ideas about what living plants, animals, and insects look like. Observational drawing is a skill that many teachers aim to sharpen in their students. It involves looking closely at the details of an object and trying to record those details as realistically as possible. For very young children, drawings will start out as scribbles or "blobs" of color. Drawing and documenting can be an exercise in creative expression. The important thing about science notebooks is the process of using them and the habit of using them as a tool for learning, not necessarily the accuracy or skill with which they are used.

Teachers who work with children in the older elementary grades will find many reasons to use science notebooks in the classroom, including their reliability as a tool for documenting children's thinking. Teachers can use them as formative assessment tools to better understand the ideas and questions that children have. Children's drawings, notes, and other jottings will help teachers make sense of their understanding and the things they are curious about.

The art and practice of keeping science notebooks can be a powerful learning tool for older children. They get practice with writing and language use, vocabulary, and organization, and they have a place to work out math problems. Elementary science notebooks are lovely tools for cross-disciplinary integration, and most teachers and students find them to be very valuable tools for learning.

In the early years, science notebooks should simply be introduced as special, enjoyable tools to help children enjoy documenting their thinking. For this reason, I refer to them as "journals" rather than notebooks, since the purpose and use of the books is slightly different from how science notebooks are generally used. Many educators think of journals as more open-ended, whereas notebooks tend to have specific objectives. Use whatever terminology you prefer.

The idea behind science journals in the early years is twofold: First, the science journal helps establish the norm that "we write and make sketches about science when we have scientific ideas or questions." This affirms the idea that writing, drawing, and keeping records is part of the act of doing science. This also helps children recognize, understand, and practice communication and representation. Children can even smear mud or soil in their journals, or press flowers or leaves, to help them remember a special time or place in nature.

Second, the science journal is a special place. Young children become very attached to their science journals, and rightfully so. Ensure that each child's treasured journal is his or her own, and that he or she is free to use it when inspired to do so. To minimize the potential heartbreak of lost journals, I suggest keeping the journals in a designated box in the classroom so that children will always know where to go to access their journals. Some teachers keep a special collection of writing tools, such as blendable colored pencils or oil pastels, to encourage children to use their journals. Most young children treasure their journals and are happy to have a place that's "all mine" for their notes and other meaningful things.

Remember, in the context of early childhood, it's not the content of the journal that matters at this point (although there is nothing wrong with providing the occasional prompt or suggestion about what the children could draw or write for those who are reluctant or seem stuck), it's the *act* of keeping a journal that's important. Engaging in that act will reinforce the habit of keeping a journal, which will support children's growth and understanding of STEM in later years.

If you wish to use science journals with the children in your class, I recommend you use journals with blank paper or composition books that have lines only on the bottom half of the page and are blank at the top, to leave room for children's illustrations. For children who are not yet writing, label the notebooks with each child's name and provide a blank piece of paper where the child can create a

This boy paints in his science journal.

cover illustration for his journal, and then cover the drawing with clear adhesive-backed paper to protect it. Consider how you will make journaling part of the daily routine. Invite children to use their journals whenever they have an idea or thought they want to write or draw about. Some teachers invite children to paste leaves, grasses, or flower petals in the pages of the journal, or provide pieces of clear adhesive-backed paper that children can use to tack items down.

USING DIGITAL TECHNOLOGY TO DOCUMENT LEARNING

In today's media-rich world, many early care and education settings have resources such as iPods, digital cameras, and other devices that they wish to incorporate into their STEM learning. These devices can serve as invitations and empowering ways for young children to document their learning, and are often seen as very special. If possible, ensure that you have enough devices for all the children to have their own, or be sure that you have established a set of norms around sharing so that every child has an equal chance to experiment with the use of digital technology for documenting learning.

A variety of apps and other digital tools help primary-aged children record images of nature.

Many educators invite children to take pictures while out in nature, and those photos can later be printed and added to a child's journal or perhaps a class portfolio. I've seen educators use photos taken by children to document the work and play that happen outdoors, and some teachers collect and organize the photos by month or by another theme. Other teachers use cameras as tools to help children direct their attention to certain elements of the natural world. One teacher invited each of her children to take a picture of moss when exploring a natural area. The teacher later printed the photos and had a beautiful collection that showed a few different species of moss the children had identified. The children were challenged to take close-up photos that depicted tiny details of the mosses, such as the star-like shape of one species and the deep velvety green fuzz of another. They created a photo gallery in their classroom to share the images and, in doing so, celebrated the children's observations.

Another teacher invited her class to "take a picture of something brown" and was treated to an assortment of photos of tree bark, rocks, dirt, stones, and dry pine needles on the forest floor. An exercise like this helps children see and think about the many different shades of a color, as well as notice details in nature they may not have previously noted. This exercise can be repeated often using different or multiple colors as the focus, which will lead to a colorful collection of nature images the children will be proud to display.

Purposeful explorations with cameras where the children have suggested items or colors to photograph can challenge children's thinking in new ways as they are encouraged to look more closely at things or shift their perspective. With iPods or other recording devices, children can record sounds and images, such as leaves blowing in the wind, butterflies visiting a flower bed, or tall grasses waving on a breezy day. You can introduce software that allows them to edit a series of photos, such as one photo taken each day of the same plant, to create beautiful time-lapse diaries of plant growth and change.

Using Questions to Guide Learning

One way to help support children's STEM learning is to use questioning techniques to help them clarify their questions, focus their attention, reflect on their thinking, and create investigations. In science we often think of these sorts of questions as "productive" questions because they propel us forward in our thinking (Etgeest 1985). They can be quite useful in helping children to narrow their attention to particular phenomena or elements of an investigation, or to take action. They help children link their thinking to their actions, and vice versa. Science educator Mary Lee Martens classifies productive questions into four categories:

1. **Attention-focusing questions** help students fix their attention on certain details. These questions help children make observations, notice and articulate details, and also help them develop the skill of discernment, the ability to attend to certain details that are more important than others. Examples: "*Have you noticed* that there are a lot of chipmunks over by the bird feeder?" "*What are* they doing?" "*What happened when* the bell rang?"

2. **Measuring and counting questions** help students make more precise, mathematically oriented observations. They help children see and think in terms of quantity and number, and they help with spatial awareness. Examples: "*How many* chipmunks are under the bird feeder?" "*How often* do we picnic by the pond?" "*How long* is this stick?" "*How many* scoops of wood chips fit into Jack's bowl?"

3. **Comparison questions** can help students analyze what they know or classify their observations or knowledge. They push children to find

Experiences with materials of different lengths, weights, and shapes help children think mathematically as they discuss their plans to build a fort.

similarities among things that may appear to be different. They also help children identify differences among things that may appear to be the same. Examples: "*How are the* chipmunks *the same as/like* the birds? *How are* they *different*?"

4. **Action questions** help students explore certain phenomena or take certain actions to lead to new information. These questions are at the heart of many investigations. Examples: "*What happens if* we clap our hands while the chipmunks are eating under the bird feeder?" "*Can you try to* make that water come out of the watering can faster?" "*Can you make* the dandelion seeds fly away?"

THE TYPES OF QUESTIONS CHILDREN ASK

One way that educators can help to drive and focus children's explorations is to think about the kinds of questions that children ask. In the seemingly infinite world of children's questions, there are several types. Science educator Wynne Harlen (2006) has identified several major categories of questions that children tend to ask. There are "why" questions: Why do the birds sing? These kinds of questions are the kind that many educators dread! Many of them seem to have no answer, or, if they do, educators may not immediately know the answer. But underneath those "why" questions are often other ideas or observations that, when shared, can lead to rich—and answerable!—questions. Listen carefully and don't dismiss "why" questions. When children ask "why," what they are often wondering is "What makes that happen?" "Why does it work this way?" "The birds were not singing last time I went outside, and they are now. What's different?"

It takes practice to gauge the underlying question behind the "why" questions. Sometimes they seem to have no answer, and other times they are evidence that a child is wondering about a process or phenomena that she can't yet articulate. For example, she may have noticed that as the weather warms, more birds are singing as she plays in the school yard in the morning. Engaging her in a conversation that would give her a chance to share these observations might help you determine what she is wondering about. Talking with her about her observation (for example, by responding with a clarifying question of your own: "You hear more birds singing this morning than you did last time we were outside—is that right?" "How can you tell?") will help hone her thinking and clarify her observation so she can identify what it is that she really is wondering about. Then you can work together to gather information or investigate phenomena. You can better understand what children are wondering by asking them additional questions about what they want to know. They are often really wondering about things that can be investigated (Harlen 2003).

Children also ask questions that are simply requests for information or facts, such as, "What is the name of that butterfly?" or "Where does the frog live?" and these questions can be answered with information if you know the answer. In many cases, teachers don't know the answer, in which case a simple "I don't know; let's see if we can find out!" is a great response (so long as you are able to spend the time investigating or can make a commitment to come back to it). Children ask these sorts of questions as they try to build context for their world and the creatures, phenomena, and objects around them. They are always busy trying to make sense of everything!

Perhaps the most challenging kinds of questions for teachers are those that require complex answers: "Why do leaves change color?" or "Why does the frog have so many spots?" These are common questions that young children ask, and there are many levels of explanation that you can provide. Teachers often feel intimidated by such questions because the "correct" answer is often complex or beyond the child's level of development. In other cases, the teacher simply may not know the correct answer. But these types of questions are full of opportunity. Rather than simply trying to answer the questions, a teacher can listen carefully to the question and identify what it is within the question that can be investigated. For example, in response to the question "Why does the frog have so many spots?" you could start a conversation about camouflage, if that seems appropriate, or instead, turn the question into one that could be investigated, simply by changing the question to "Do all frogs have so many spots?" or "How many spots does that frog have?" There are a lot of ways to investigate that question. Turning questions in this way takes practice. It may be helpful to think about connecting some action to your question. For example, it's hard to think of an action associated with "Why does the frog have so many spots?" but changing the question to one that could involve counting, comparing, or other STEM skills can help you determine how to investigate that question. When you hear a question and you think it's a good opportunity to investigate further, ask yourself, *What can we learn about* _____? *How can we learn about* _____? *What can we change or do to learn more about* _____? As you reflect on these questions, you will likely come up with specific ideas for investigation.

Using Materials to Spur STEM Thinking

Children are constantly inspired to express themselves, and there are many ways that teachers can support that inspiration. Guiding questions, new experiences, and new materials will all inspire children to represent their ideas. If children have been using clay or dough to make small animals in the art area, why not introduce mud as a new creative medium? It may lead to discoveries about the properties of mud versus clay and experimentation with tools in a new way, and it may also provide children with new ways to make observations about the objects they want to represent.

A child uses mud as a medium for painting. She thins it out with water to change the color and consistency.

For example, if the mud is very gritty but a child wants to make her snake smooth and shiny, she will notice the difference right away. She will need to figure out how to change the consistency of the material so that she can make it fit her needs. Other ways that educators can create a STEM-rich environment include collecting intriguing items from nature or tools that children will be familiar with: garden implements such as shovels, trowels, and seed cups. You can take plants from outdoors and bring them indoors or set up temporary housing for creatures gently captured during an outdoor excursion.

BOOKS

Providing books, photographs, and other reference materials related to things that children have noticed or expressed interest in can revive waning interests or provide new information for ongoing investigations. Some teachers use books to introduce new ideas or concepts as well. For example, one class had been spending a lot of time outdoors investigating ladybugs. By this point in the year, the children knew where to find them and what plants they would like in their garden to attract more ladybugs and other insects. The teacher wanted to expand their focus to include additional plants and insects, so she brought in some new books that focused on milkweed beetles and other insects the children were likely to encounter. She also brought in photos and books about common plants that they might want to add to their garden as well. For children's outdoor excursions, she printed up cards depicting common butterflies and other pollinators. The children carried the "field guides" with them on an outdoor butterfly hunt.

Changes in environment can also be provocative STEM starts. When you go outside at various times of the day, children will begin to notice different patterns of light, temperature, and weather. They may notice different noise levels—for example, the noise of birdsong or lively children in the morning at drop-off time versus the relative quiet of midafternoon. Be sure to visit the outdoors in all seasons and at different times of the day so that children may experience changes in temperature, noise levels, and light levels. This will help them see nature in new and different ways.

This girl identifies insects with the help of a card her teacher created.

Creating a Community of Curiosity

Most educators of young children could easily describe a literacy-rich classroom, because for many years there has been a strong push nation-wide to support early literacy. Although each teacher has his own interpretation of what *literacy-rich* might mean, most classrooms have a lot in common in this regard. Some teachers support literacy-rich classrooms by providing print materials at every opportunity, such as books, magazines, labels, and other print media. Cozy reading areas in class-rooms provide a place for children to engage with print materials to satisfy their own curiosity, learn quietly, and be alone or in small groups, and enjoy books and words. "Listening stations" where children can listen to books or other stories on CD or MP3 players provide a place for children to hear oral sto-ries, thereby experiencing the pleasure of storytelling. Read-aloud is the favorite time of day for many children (and teachers!), and it provides a time for children to experience new words, practice reading comprehension, and learn about the cadence and rhythms of speech—all important language arts skills. Classroom writing centers offer children a place to play and practice holding pens, cray-ons, markers, pencils, and other tools and writing technology. They may prac-tice using these tools on enticing notepads, message pads, lined and gridded papers, colorful papers, fancy printed papers, small blank notebooks, dry erase boards, chalkboards, and other surfaces. Typewriters and computers offer two additional examples of technology that we use for writing and reading. Some teachers provide stencils, magnetic letters, sandpaper letters, or other materials that invite children to explore the shapes of letters and how they look alongside one another. This is a great example of how literacy is taught in a very integrated way. Many teachers are very comfortable and fluent in seizing opportunities to harness children's natural curiosities about the written and spoken word, and the result is an integration of literacy that clearly supports children's learning in a profound way.

Read-alouds outdoors help connect nature and STEM to language arts.

One of the things that has made the push for early literacy so successful has been the level at which it has been integrated across the curriculum, the physical spaces, and the daily routine of children. Language arts permeates most classrooms. Teachers have developed great skill at drawing out the literacy connections in many areas and seizing the many opportunities that arise naturally throughout the day for children to think about things using a "literacy lens"—in other words, using their growing understanding of the written word, of language, and in the ways that they use words and letters to process their experiences.

Integration at this level recognizes that there are many *places* for learning, *ways* of learning, and *catalysts* for learning (Iman, Trundle, et al. 2010). Subjects must be integrated for them to have the most meaning and the greatest impact. We don't learn language as a separate discipline, it's a tool that helps us understand the world and through it, our experiences are enriched.

STEM should be regarded in the same way. I believe that educators can create *STEM-rich* environments for early learners that are equally integrated and with the potential to have just as significant an impact on children's learning and perspective about the subject. Consider what this might look like in your setting: where are the young child's places for learning STEM? Can STEM be woven throughout the curriculum much like literacy? What about the classroom and outdoor environments? How can we make those STEM-rich? What would children's daily routines look like if STEM were integrated?

Researchers suggest that elements such as peer culture, play, activity, and the culture of the classroom are also important catalysts for learning. They cite the significance of a "set of common activities, routines, artifacts, concerns, values, and attitudes constructed and shared by a group of children," in other words, the culture created and maintained by the children themselves (Iman, Trundle, et al. 2010). Peer culture is an environment where children work *together* to develop ideas and construct knowledge. It is an environment in which taking intellectual risks is valued, encouraged, and supported, and where children share artifacts (collections of objects that have meaning to them, such as items from nature) and use them as prompts for discourse and tools in their knowledge construction. How can you create such an environment in your own classroom? How do you create conditions so that students can take intellectual risks together in the pursuit of knowledge?

Classroom cultures that support spontaneous, collaborative, open-ended, and extended investigation of the things children are curious about are cultures that support STEM learning. These characteristics of a learning climate could describe an early childhood classroom or a working engineering or science laboratory. It's through creative discourse and interaction with one's peers, as well as collaborating to find meaning based on experience, that new discoveries are made! Of course, by now you know the value of creating a classroom environment that welcomes intellectual and physical risk taking, questions, trial and error, and open-

A STEM-rich environment offers many connections between and among disciplines.

ended investigation. Children engage in STEM through play, collaboration, and investigation of materials.

Research suggests that there are numerous ways teachers can help children in cocreating knowledge and collectively engaging in a classroom community that supports STEM learning. In fact, STEM learning itself can contribute to a cohesive classroom community, since the social, collaborative nature of inquiry and engaging together in investigation helps build relationships and investment in learning. Children can develop confidence in their ability to solve problems and cooperate with one another. They know their feelings, ideas, and questions are valued (VanMeeteren and Zan 2010).

Conclusion

My hope is that this book offers you new insight into the many ways in which children are naturally inclined to engage in STEM-related learning. Their tendencies to immerse themselves in the habits of mind and practices of STEM make it a natural fit for early childhood settings. Nature offers an abundance of resources to teachers who want to connect nature-based learning with STEM learning. From the loose parts and open spaces to explore to the variety of textures, materials, and sensory stimuli available for children and adults to be curious about, the natural world offers plenty of material

A STEM-centered classroom values investigation, collaboration, and a lot of outdoor play!

and opportunities for STEM learning. Give children plenty of occasions to play in nature and you will see their peer relationships strengthen, and their intrapersonal skills such as confidence and self-efficacy grow, and you will see them engaged in the practices we associate with STEM.

I also hope this book has given you specific examples of the many opportunities you can use within nature-based settings to jump into STEM investigations and exploration. You don't need to add anything to your curriculum—many rich resources are already available to you and the children in your care. Children are already engaging in the fundamental practices associated with STEM. Children's natural curiosity about the environment and the creatures who live there means that there will be no shortage of questions and opportunities for curiosity, investigation, and joy. Likewise there will be no shortage of reasons to spend extended periods of time outdoors in nature-based settings. I hope that you will do it frequently, and with a new confidence in nature's intrinsic value as well as its potential to impact children's natural tendencies to "think STEM." Thank you for the work that you do to engage children with the natural world. What you do matters.

Children are naturally curious about the materials they find in nature.

STEM Starts

6

THIS CHAPTER CONTAINS STEM STARTS OUTLINING connections between and among disciplines, as well as connections to the basic scientific concepts I call the Big Ideas. These are the areas of content that are appropriate for the early years. Don't be too concerned about knowing all the details of these content areas. In the early years, we aim to help children build their investigative skills within these contexts. Robin Moore, a landscape architect specializing in children's nature places, coined the term *affordances* to refer to "entry points" into an activity or form of play (Zamani and Moore 2013). This section contains affordances for children to investigate STEM ideas and concepts, as well as to learn the thinking skills and practices of STEM.

In most cases, the suggested activities will easily address more than one of the STEM domains, depending on how you and the children focus your attention and what direction you take the activity. You will find that each STEM start contains opportunities for children to engage in a number of the practices discussed in this book, so you can adapt them to suit your needs and the children's interests. The activities are open-ended enough for you to use the children's interest as a jumping-off point to address whatever scientific topics are appropriate for that particular time and context.

There are plenty of opportunities for children to explore counting, size, shape, measurement, weight, heft, and balance in this collection of tree stumps.

Connecting to the Big Ideas

In early childhood, repeated visits to an idea—as well as a place—through play and investigation will do a lot to help children build knowledge and make meaning from their world. The following chart identifies some "big ideas" that are appropriate for children in early childhood. Many, if not all, of your outdoor explorations will center around one or more of these big ideas.

	Big Idea topic	Examples
	Living things and life cycles	Characteristics of living and nonliving things, human health, parts and systems of living things, the interaction of living things with their environment (what things eat, how they interact with one another, interdependence and relatedness).
	Earth and space	Ecosystems, water systems, Earth's relationship to other planets, stars, causes of seasons, landforms, geology.
	Materials, structure and function	The diversity and variety of materials and structures made from materials, including human-made (e.g., papers, plastics, simple machines) and natural materials (e.g., rocks, soil, water, as well as their attributes).
	Air and weather	These concepts are somewhat abstract, but hands-on experiences with temperature changes, moving air, and seasons helps make them tangible.
	Forces and motion	Starting, stopping, pushing, pulling, falling, floating, and other movements; transportation and other systems; and simple machines.
	Energy and matter	Energy can be defined as the ability to make things happen or change. Examples include heat, light, electricity, and motion.

LIVING THINGS AND LIFE CYCLES

Investigations of living things and life cycles includes experiences with plants, animals, human health and bodies, as well as with parts and systems within living things and nature. Investigations include how living things interact with and depend on one another as well as how they are affected by the environment.

Children have a lot of questions about plants and trees. Many children know that trees and plants are alive, but they don't yet understand how something so different from humans and animals can also be alive. Plants provide a perfect jumping-off point for investigations about living and nonliving things—important ideas that form the basis of many science standards for the early grades. In fact, one common misconception children express when talking about plants is that if they drop their leaves or turn brown, "they are dead." Children may not know that many plants (including trees) enter a state of dormancy during the winter, but they are not dead. Their leaves stop producing chlorophyll (which gives them their characteristic green color), their flowers stop producing seeds, and many plants drop their leaves. The plant's energy is concentrated in the roots during this time, and during the colder months, the roots of the plant are busy obtaining nutrients from the soil.

EARTH AND SPACE

During the early childhood years, encouraging a sense of wonder and curiosity about outer space, including the stars and moon, is critical for helping inspire later learning in these areas. Listen and record their observations and questions. Encouraging families in your program to venture outdoors at night to stargaze will also help deepen children's curiosity. As children explore and investigate earth materials such as rocks, water, sand, and gravel, they are building experience with the matter that makes up the earth. Explorations of earth and space will likely include investigations of ecosystems; water and water systems; earth materials like sand, mud, and rocks; Earth's relationship to other planets and stars; causes of seasons; and landforms and geology.

While the concepts of space and distance are a bit complex for young children, they are very much in tune with tangible things related to Earth and space, such as the sun, stars, and moon, as well as Earth. While most young children will understand that a globe or a map is a representation of "this place where we live"—creating maps or really understanding the scale involved can be very challenging for young children. Helping to connect them with their own environment, such as their school yard and their neighborhood, will help to create a foundation for a map of "home" that grows as they age. Understanding that Earth is part of a larger system is something that they will understand later, and experiences with other systems (such as water systems, trees, plants, and animals) will help them generalize their understanding later.

MATERIALS, STRUCTURE AND FUNCTION

Children build understanding of materials whenever they are playing, exploring, getting dirty, and engaging in a hands-on way with materials, whether natural or human-made. You can help deepen their learning by asking them questions that bring their attention to characteristics of materials, such as hard, soft, shiny, rough. They can experiment with how different materials can be manipulated, such as when water is added to soil. Some materials can be broken or bent, and that will affect their structure as well as their function. As children become more and more familiar with and gain experience using different kinds of materials, they will make decisions about the best kind of materials for certain jobs. This is particularly useful in engineering where children have a lot of opportunities to make informed choices about their building materials. Conversation about the characteristics of materials will help them classify materials and build a reserve of knowledge that will be useful in much of their work.

Structure and function relates directly to materials, because as children build with materials, they develop an understanding of their structure and function and how they use them to create things that also have a structure and function (such as a stick fort). Children also learn about structure and function when they look closely at animals and insects, investigating their body structures through observation or touch. They gain a sense of the structure and function of plant parts through playing with them as loose parts, hiding in and among them, touching them, and looking closely at them.

Children learn about systems when they have experiences with parts of a whole, are able to relate the part to the whole, and understand its function within that larger system. For example, a child makes a connection that leaves are parts of a tree and that the leaf has a role in keeping that system alive (by making food for the tree). Sand play at a beach is another opportunity to engage in experience with systems: as children create rivulets and streams that flow into larger streams, they are creating miniature water systems. Another opportunity to learn about systems comes when children create them, such as a system to move water from one place to another with tubes and buckets, or a system made up of levers and ramps to help them move heavy rocks. In using the systems, they come to understand that all parts are important in keeping the system working. Hands on investigations may include the diversity and variety of materials and structures made from materials, including human-made (e.g., papers, plastics, simple machines) and natural materials (e.g., rocks, soil, water, as well as their attributes).

AIR AND WEATHER

Playing in all sorts of weather will provide lots of opportunities to experience and explore air, weather, and temperature; experimenting with flying objects and objects that move in air; looking at the effects of wind; and building experiences with moving air, how air moves things, and how things can be moved by air. Since weather is closely related to air, experiencing all types of weather is important for children (within the limits of safety, of course), and most teachers who use the outdoors frequently go beyond simply "naming" the weather each day. Find out what you can about rain, sunshine, snow, and crisp autumn breezes by being outside and looking for evidence of the weather's effect on things. Can you find frost on the grasses? Does the surface of a puddle freeze? All of these exciting discoveries will lead to deeper investigation and meaning-making. Investigations may also include hands-on experiences with temperature changes and moving air; and seasons help make experiences tangible. Investigations of sound are related to air, since sound waves travel through air as vibrations.

Air is made up of oxygen, nitrogen, and other gases. It's key to life on Earth. Air creates a layer around our planet called the atmosphere, where air flows and swirls constantly, redistributing heat and moisture around the globe. The atmosphere is hundreds of miles thick, and within it are several different layers. Within the troposphere, the layer closest to the earth, is where the weather occurs. The air in our atmosphere can vary greatly in temperature. The sun's rays warm the air, but they do so unevenly, heating areas in different locations differently (for example, the areas near the equator are heated more than the earth's poles). Warmer air rises, thus moving the air around the atmosphere constantly. Air also exerts a small amount of pressure on everything, due to its weight. This pressure results in constant change. When air moves from places of high pressure to low pressure, we experience wind. The movement of air and air pressure cause the conditions of weather that we experience on a day-to-day basis.

FORCE AND MOTION

Young children are constantly experimenting with forces they create as well as those they observe. They push and pull, roll and drop, fill and dump, balance and fall. These are all firsthand experiences with force and motion, and this is the knowledge-building material that children need to create understanding of physics and physical science. When they investigate the materials they use in making things move or fit together, they are also learning more about systems: how things work together, as "parts-of-a-whole." These investigations also give them a chance to practice their spatial reasoning as they consider *positionality*, or where things are in space and in relation to other objects. Simple machines are a classic topic for helping children develop an understanding of force and motion, and a topic that is found in many early care and education settings. Investigations may include starting, stopping, pushing, pulling, falling, floating, and other movements; transportation and other systems; and simple machines.

Forces act on objects all the time. Gravity is the force that attracts things to earth. When you throw a ball into the air, gravity is what makes it return to the ground. But there are lots of other forces that affect the motion of objects. For example, when a ball rolls along the ground, it may appear to stop all by itself, when in reality the force of the ground and the air acting on the ball are what cause it to stop rolling. Many forces and their effects are "invisible" and difficult for young learners to understand and integrate into their knowledge construction.

ENERGY AND MATTER

Energy is everywhere. Generally speaking, anything that's moving is using something called "kinetic energy"—the energy of motion. There is another kind of energy called "potential energy," which refers to the energy stored within something (think of a rubber band stretched tight). Within those two categories are additional types of energy. In early childhood settings, when we talk about energy, we are usually describing the capacity of something to move, grow, change, or do work.

Matter is any substance that occupies space and that has mass. All matter is made up of atoms, some of the tiniest building blocks in the universe. Generally speaking, there are three main states of matter: solids, liquids, and gasses.

Energy is described as the capacity to do work. There are several types of energy, including mechanical, heat energy, chemical, electrical, and even gravitational energy. Energy is what makes things change. Your investigations of energy might include explorations of how things (such as water, living things, and so on) move, grow, and change. Matter is anything that takes up space and has mass: any kind of material is matter, even air (even though you can't see it!).

Crosscutting Concepts

Another resource that may be helpful for you is the set of "cross cutting concepts" articulated in the Next Generation Science Standards. They are concepts that link one or more content areas together, often reaching across disciplines. As discussed earlier, integration of the STEM disciplines is important, and there are lots of opportunities to make connections between and among the Big Ideas, practices, and crosscutting concepts listed here. The result will be a meaningful and richly integrated experience with STEM. The chart in appendix D may be helpful.

Opportunities to introduce these crosscutting concepts can be found within topics that are typically already being addressed in many early childhood settings. For example, during the autumn season, a teacher might focus on pumpkins. Within that broad topic of pumpkins, the students might at times be investigating patterns (such as the pattern of a pumpkin's skin, the symmetry in its stem, or the leaves on the pumpkin vine), or structures and function (of the plant and the pumpkin itself), stability and change (as they observe it aging and rotting away), as well as scale and quantity. Within each of the topics listed below are numerous developmentally appropriate ways to use the crosscutting concepts to help link material to STEM.

Remember that in early childhood, simply unearthing children's thinking and listening to their ideas is the important first step toward engaging in a path of discovery that will serve them well for years to come. While it is tempting to do as many activities as possible, remember that when children are really engaged in learning and play, investigation and exploration can often keep their attention for quite some time. Please be sure to allow plenty of time for the children to immerse themselves in their investigations. Their understanding will result from immersion in their investigations of phenomena, reflection (such as documenting their observations), engaging in discourse with their peers, and integrating the experience, contributions, and ideas that others have shared.

Appendix A, "Resources for Increasing Your STEM Understanding," provides a list of ideas for you to increase your own understanding beyond what is in the scope of this book.

Crosscutting Concepts

Patterns

Observed patterns in nature, such as shapes, sizes, and even events, guide organization and classification and prompt questions about relationships and causes underlying them.

Cause and effect

Events have causes, sometimes simple, sometimes complex. Scientists and engineers think a lot about what makes things happen and why.

Scale, proportion, and quantity

In considering phenomena, it is critical to recognize what is relevant at different size, time, and energy scales, and to recognize proportional relationships between difference quantities as scales change.

Systems and system models

A system is an organized group of related objects or components; models can be used for understanding and predicting the behavior of systems.

Energy and matter

Tracking energy and matter flows into, out of, and within systems helps one understand their system's behavior.

Structure and function

The way an object is shaped or structured determines many of its properties and functions.

Stability and change

For both designed and natural systems, conditions that affect stability and factors that control rates of change are critical elements to consider and understand.

(NSTA 2013) http://ngss.nsta.org/crosscuttingconceptsfull.aspx

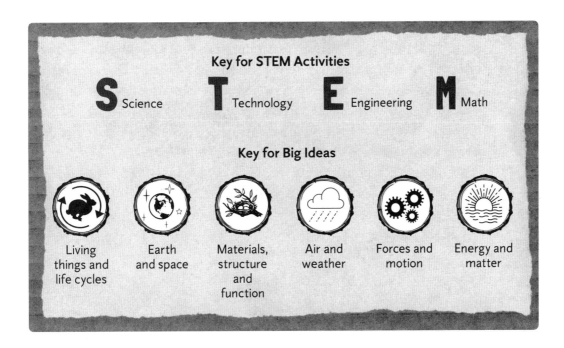

Key for STEM Activities

S Science **T** Technology **E** Engineering **M** Math

Key for Big Ideas

Living things and life cycles Earth and space Materials, structure and function Air and weather Forces and motion Energy and matter

STEM Starts

You will see that, like the STEM starts sprinkled throughout the book, these are not step-by-step activities. Since the important thing about STEM in the early years is to build fluency and comfort with the key practices, I provide these ideas only as jumping-off points for you to start your investigations. It is up to you and your expertise to determine how deeply, and in which direction, to take any of these STEM starts. As mentioned previously, each of these activities will address one or more of the STEM domains and will also lead to engagement in many of the practices described in this book. That is the beauty of the STEM starts—their inherent flexibility. The guiding questions provided in each activity help deepen children's engagement and focus their observations.

Perhaps you have heard children making observations about some of the topics here and you want some ideas for increasing the STEM focus. Use the questioning techniques outlined in chapter 5's "Using Questions to Guide Learning." Or, if you are engaged in an investigation about one thing, scan the STEM starts to determine if there is anything that you could add to increase children's interest and deepen their learning or take it in a new direction. Encourage the children's questions and observations, and let those point your way to your investigations.

1

STEM
Start

Capitalize on young children's interest in animals by inviting them to represent animals they might find in the natural areas near your school. Provide materials for them to represent their thinking: invite them to draw, paint, create from wire, or sculpt from mud and clay found outdoors. Use this time as a way to create fanciful, imaginary animals. Then, bring in photos you or they have taken of animals in the school's natural places. Look closely at the animal's body, fur or feathers, color, number of legs, eyes, and other characteristics. Ask children to list as many attributes as they can. Continue to make materials available for their creations.

2

STEM
Start

Compare attributes of animals by identifying visible characteristics, such as fur, hooves, four legs versus two, feathers, beaks, sharp teeth. Discuss how they are alike or different. Create groups or categories based on attributes. How do you think these specific attributes help animals? What makes you think so?

3

STEM
Start

Encourage students to share evidence that supports the idea that living things grow (such as animals, pets, or their peers). How do they know? Ask them to think about changes (in size, weight, appearance, and abilities). If they compare a variety of animals, they can begin to make generalizations about what it means to be a living thing and to grow.

4

In your excursions outdoors, gather the children to sit quietly and be very still. (This will take some practice!) Aim for five minutes or so. This will help them direct their attention to what they can hear, smell, see, and feel. If you make this a regular practice, children will be able to do it for longer periods. Sitting quietly is a great way to tune in to nature and create a sense of calm. Breathe deeply and slowly. It's a great practice for all children and can be very helpful for children prone to anxiety or hyperactivity.

5

How do you know what animals need? Ask the children what animals need to survive. Gather information by making observations. What will you need to observe to make conclusions about what animals need? Look at areas such as a bird feeding station, gardens, and nests. How do you know that an animal lives somewhere? What evidence do you have? Children will likely identify nests, tracks (if done in winter or wet weather), trails formed by animals through grasses, evidence of chewing (such as chewed shrubs or bark, leaves with holes, or piles of debris [called *middens*] from a squirrel's feast on nuts).

6

How could you make a home for an animal? Use natural materials to create animal homes. What elements are important to include? What animal could use the home you are making? Leave your animal homes outdoors and visit them periodically to see if you can find evidence that animals have been investigating!

7

STEM
Start

Children love to collect earthworms. Invite them to gently do so and corral them in a pie pan or other spot where you can observe them closely. What can the children tell you about their bodies? Provide hand lenses and other tools for them to use. How do the worms move? Which end is the front? How do you know? How are worms alike, and how are they different? Do they all look the same? Children will likely notice that the worms are "slimy" or "shiny," that they have moist skin, no legs, feel cool, and move by pulling themselves along with tiny hairs, or *cilia*, on the outside of their bodies.

8

STEM
Start

How and where can you find earthworms? Compare the different areas where you have observed worms after a rainstorm. If you wanted to collect worms for observation, where would you find them? What is the same or different about those locations? What are the best tools for digging for worms? Do the tools need to change depending on any other factors, such as weather or dampness of soil? After doing this investigation regularly, ask the children if there are some places that are better than others for collecting. If so, what makes them better? Why do you think the worms prefer those areas?

9

STEM
Start

Find other creatures living in your region that can be safely collected: crayfish, ants, caterpillars, ladybugs, spiders, pill bugs (also known as "roly polies"). If you have a body of water nearby, get out the dip nets and a few white dishpans (white makes it easier to see the creatures inside) and collect creatures from the water. Examine their sizes, shapes, body coverings, movement, and behavior.

10
STEM Start

Use a variety of colors of dishpans (including white) or other containers to hold water that you and the children have collected from the nearby pond or stream. Provide flashlights so that children can look in to the pans. Are the microorganisms easier to see in dishpans of one color rather than another? What tools can you use to investigate the tiny creatures that live in the water? Could you invent a tool that would help you investigate?

Important! If you collect and house insects or other animals temporarily, be sure to keep the containers out of direct sunlight and return the animals gently to the place where you found them immediately after your investigation is complete. Also, never use soap or cleaning products to wash containers or collecting equipment. The chemicals are much too harsh for the critters you're collecting and can contaminate water as well. And keep the containers in a special location that's clearly marked "no food use" so that they are reserved for nature experiences.

11
STEM Start

Find a shady, moist location that has fallen trees or logs. Roll a log over and see what critters are underneath. There are usually all sorts of animals under logs, such as spiders, worms, millipedes, mites, and pill bugs. Children will enjoy watching them and will likely be fascinated by the fact that the creatures live and find shelter under logs. Compare the creatures you find and note their characteristics. How are they alike, and how are they different? How many different species do you see? Take photos if you can, and when you return inside, invite the children to draw, paint, or create from clay the different creatures they found. Many children will want to re-create the whole scene; many will wish to draw just one creature. You may consider making a diorama together with a shoe box and paper or other materials.

12

STEM Start

Insects belong to the phylum Arthropoda, which are animals characterized by a segmented body, jointed limbs, no backbone, and an exoskeleton (external skeleton). Children will be able to see that segmented body more easily with some insects than with others. They will also likely note that insects have antennae, three pairs of legs, and wings. Rather than you pointing out these features directly, use guiding questions to draw their attention to these observations; this will take time and repeated visits to the insect world. Take the time to build a list or record data in your journals of "what we have observed about insects."

13

STEM Start

Select a shrub or flowering plant in the school's natural area. Pay daily visits to the plant and make observations about it. Ask the children how they would like to record the plant's growth (for example, through using units such as paper clips or a tape measure to measure) or by documenting it in photographs or drawings each day. Visiting the same plant again and again will tune them in to subtle changes in height, number and frequency of buds, leaf growth, and how it changes over time as the seasons pass. You can do this with a variety of plants. Such observations really help young children gain a tangible sense of long-term change, which can sometimes be a difficult concept to grasp.

14 STEM Start

Venture outdoors with hand lenses and other tools to compare leaf shapes. If you have a lot of space, it can be helpful to section off an area by placing a hula hoop or ribbon on the ground and focusing on what's inside. Look closely at the diversity of plant shapes, colors, and whether or not they all have flowers. What do the green leaves have in common? How are they different? What words can you use to describe the shape of a blade of grass or the leaf of a violet? Do the leaves have smooth edges, jagged edges, or something else? What are the tallest plants? What are the smallest plants? Children may be inspired to count the different species they can observe or to draw or paint them. Some children will want to pick a plant or two and include it in their science journals using tape or clear adhesive paper.

15 STEM Start

Set up a bird feeding station. Many children are delighted by birds and love to watch them forage in the wild. You can set up a bird feeding area near your classroom so that children can get an up close look. What kinds of feeders work best? Tray feeders, basket feeders, tube feeders? Do some research together using the Internet or books, and find out how you can build your own feeders—for example, by bending wire mesh into a box shape or filling a nylon stocking with thin, tiny seeds that birds can pull from its fibers. How else could you make feeders? Provide logs, hand drills, and sunflower butter, and see what kind of creations the children invent. You can also experiment with different ways of providing water for the birds.

Note: Avoid using peanut butter for bird feeders and ensure that your birdseed is peanut-free to be inclusive of children with nut allergies. Often the nuts in birdseeds are enough to cause an allergic reaction.

16
STEM Start

As you observe birds at the feeders or elsewhere, keep track of their attributes, such as color, size, beak shape, song, and perching habits. Observe what kinds of birds prefer certain kinds of foods. Work together to create a graphic organizer, such as a tally chart, graph, or list of the birds and their characteristics. Watch the birds as the seasons change. Do you see any new species over time? What do you notice about the way birds move and fly? The way they eat? Drink? Binoculars are often challenging and frustrating for very young children, but older children can get the hang of how to use them if shown properly.

17
STEM Start

Get some practice with binoculars. They make a great tool for getting up close and personal with nature. But they are often frustrating to use if you aren't sure how to adjust or focus them. Here's how to adjust binoculars: First, hold them up to your eyes and adjust the width by opening or closing the binoculars. You should see one clear image. Next, close your right eye and bring the binoculars to your eyes. Look through your left eye and the eyepiece to focus on an object. Rotate the center knob or focusing wheel until that object is in clear, crisp focus. Open your right eye and adjust the focus again. Higher-end binoculars also have a rotating wheel around the right eye piece. If this is the kind you have, after focusing on an image with your left eye, close your left eye, focus on that same object with your right eye, and adjust the rotating wheel (called the *diopter adjuster*). When looking at birds or other animals, spot the animal, and then keep your eyes on it while you lift the binoculars to your face. Many "children's" binoculars are of poor quality and often cannot even be adjusted. If possible, invest in some sets of small binoculars. They will be of reasonable quality and will spare you and your students a lot of frustration!

18
STEM Start

Mammals can be found almost everywhere! Common mammals that are easy for children to spot include (in my region) gray squirrels, rabbits, and chipmunks. In less urban locations, deer are common. What mammals are common to your area? Ask the children what they know about mammals and which mammals may be found near your program site or school. Mammals are characterized by the fact that they live on land, they have a backbone and internal skeleton, they have hair or fur, and they produce milk to feed their young. Finally, they bear their young alive, not in a larval stage or as eggs. Find out what evidence children have for their understanding about mammals. Compare attributes of mammals, such as color, number of legs (four or two), habitat, and so on. Make a chart or graphic organizer to keep a record of the mammals you see in your school grounds.

19
STEM Start

If you live near the sea, collect shells and use them in your nature play. Children will naturally sort them, make patterns, seriate them (order them from smallest to largest or lightest to darkest) or sort them in other ways.

20
STEM Start

Older children (grades K–2) really enjoy mapmaking. Invite them to map the school's natural area, including paths and edges. You may also invite them to map out small sections of the overall landscape to help them refine their skills of observation and attention to detail. Engage the class in a discussion about which features they included, how they decided to include those features, and what they left out. Encourage idea sharing and learning from one another.

21
STEM Start

Take time each day to note the position of the sun. If you have a sundial, visit it and take note of the shadow. Maybe your class would like to create a sundial. A sundial is a flat plate with a pointer that can tell you what time it is based on the sun's apparent position in the sky. As the hours pass, the sun casts a shadow on different parts of the sundial. What would be the best location?

22
STEM Start

Trace your own shadows on the sidewalk with chalk. Return to the same spot during different times of the day and note how your shadows change. Do they move? Stay the same? Grow smaller or larger? As with sundials, the sun casts a different shadow depending on the time of day and its apparent position in the sky. So your shadow will look different depending on what time of day you are outdoors.

23
STEM Start

Where are the areas that receive the most sun and shade each day? Spend a lot of time outdoors near and around your natural area and note the differences and similarities about the locations that receive sun and shade. What causes shade? Use thermometers and other tools to compare differences in temperature in different locations at different times of day. What is different about the locations? Do different measuring tools produce the same result? Do all thermometers produce the same result? Does a digital thermometer register the same temperature as a mercury thermometer?

24
STEM
Start

Explore the landscape. Is the natural area at your school hilly or flat? Somewhere in between? Are there streams, ponds, or other water features? Where do they start? Where do they go? Do they join any other bodies of water? Explore the grounds and learn about the terrain. Do this during each season. If you live in a climate where the trees lose their leaves in winter, you will find that the landscape reveals a lot about itself when there are no leaves to obscure the view. If you live in an area with a lot of sand or soft soil, can you manipulate the shape of the terrain?

25
STEM
Start

What kind of rocks are children interested in? Collect rocks from a variety of natural areas or bring in rock samples. Compare and contrast the texture, size, color, shape, and weight of the rocks. What other attributes can you identify? How might you sort rocks? Invite children to create patterns and structures out of rocks. Can they balance rocks on one another? Ask them to sort the rocks into groups and then tell you why they sorted the way they did.

26
STEM
Start

How can you learn more about rocks? People who study rocks use tools like nails to scratch rocks to determine how soft or hard they are. They might break them with rock hammers to see what's inside. They look very closely at tiny details using magnifiers. There are three main types of rock: igneous, metamorphic, and sedimentary. All rocks are made of minerals. Field guides and websites will help you understand the differences and characteristics of each kind of rock. Create charts or graphic organizers to help you group and describe your rocks.

27
STEM
Start

Minerals also have identifiable characteristics. Minerals can be identified by color, size, shape, and even by the way that they break (called *cleavage*). Sometimes scientists use sharp nails to scratch them to see how hard they are. Another hardness test is to scrape the mineral on a glass plate or tile to see if it leaves a scratch or a colored streak. What are other ways that you can investigate minerals? Again, use field guides and websites to learn more about how to identify minerals and what kind of tools you'll need in your classroom.

28
STEM
Start

Soil is made up of a lot of organic material, such as leaf litter, and inorganic material, such as sand or small stones. Take soil samples by scooping soil into a container, then looking closely at what's inside the sample. Use magnifiers or a document camera to examine more closely. Select samples from different areas and compare and contrast them.

29
STEM
Start

Soil's texture, weight, and consistency change when it gets wet. Experiment with different amounts of water to make wet mud. Then see what happens if you add dry materials such as grasses, sand, or straw. What are the different types of mud good for? How can you use the mud in your building projects? Some birds use mud to hold their nests together.

30
STEM Start

Observe the effects of the wind as it moves through leaves and over grasses or dry, dusty soil. Wind is caused by the movement of warm air currents across the earth. As it moves, it sometimes picks up small particles and dust. There are tools to measure and learn about wind. A weather vane is a light-weight pointer that spins and points in the direction that the wind is blowing. An anemometer is a tool that is used to measure the speed of wind. You can find images and instructions for creating your own anemometer and weather vanes online, or you could brainstorm new ideas and ways to measure the wind. What tools could you invent for learning more about wind? What would you like to investigate?

31
STEM Start

How could you learn more about the way that flowing water moves? Streams, creeks, and rivers, even streets after a heavy rain present opportunities to investigate moving water. Children can drop lightweight objects into the water and watch what happens. Ribbons and yarn can be tied to sticks and used as measuring tools. What other ways can you investigate moving water? Scientists measure the rate of water flow in cubic feet per second, and you can go online to your local water management agency to learn more about how it's done. Why might we concern ourselves with this information? What can it tell us?

32
STEM Start

If you don't have access to a beach, shallow dishpans filled with damp sand and gravel can be used to create models of streams. Allow children to play in the sand and create hills, valleys, and other features such as ditches, river-beds, and ponds. Provide spray bottles for water as well as buckets of water so they can explore how water can impact landforms.

33
STEM
Start

Sometimes water looks cloudy or dirty, and sometimes it looks clear and clean. The reason for this is sediment, or tiny particles of dust, soil, and other matter that is washed downstream. Collect a variety of water samples in clear containers and allow time for the sediment to settle. Sometimes this can take hours! Observe what happens and what changes you can identify.

34
STEM
Start

If you live in a climate where water freezes in the winter, enlist the children's help in collecting chunks of ice. (You can also make ice cubes in the freezer.) Place them in different locations—some sunny, others shady—and observe changes to the ice over time. Will it melt? Why do you think so? Will the ice melt at the same rate or different rates in other locations?

35
STEM
Start

Invite each child to search for and select a special rock. After all the children have collected their rocks, gather together and invite everyone to share the details about their rocks, including where they found them, what shape they are, and other attributes and information that make their rocks special. Provide modeling clay or wire and invite them to re-create their rocks with these or other materials. Allowing them time to sketch their rocks on paper will prompt them to observe fine details.

36

STEM Start

Water play is a favorite outdoor play activity. Provide tools, such as containers in a variety of shapes and sizes, tubes, funnels, ramps, and scoops, so that children can move water. Encourage children to create systems that move water from one place to another. Point out how water takes the shape of whatever container it's in, a characteristic of all liquids. Encourage them to experiment with how they can use water to move things, such as leaves or other lightweight loose parts. Challenge them to experiment with making the water move slowly or quickly by changing the way they pour or add water to the system.

37

STEM Start

A pulley is a simple machine that makes moving heavy loads easier. A rope is placed over the pulley and attached to an object. When you pull on the other end of the rope, the pulley helps lift the object. Place pulleys with ropes over tree branches and use them to help lift bird feeders, heavy logs, and other materials.

38

STEM Start

Ramps help children gain experience with force and motion. When a ball is rolled down a ramp, the speed at which it rolls is related to the steepness of the ramp. Provide pieces of wood, logs, and rocks for children to create their own ramps, some steep, others more gradual. Encourage them to explore the differences in speed, distance, and force that their various ramps illustrate. How might you measure the differences?

39

STEM
Start

Sieves, egg beaters, slotted spoons, and other kitchen tools allow children to gain experience with properties of materials and tools at the same time. They can experiment with different tools and natural materials to understand the strengths and function of each type of tool. For example, some tools will work well for moving sand; others won't. Some tools will be useful for sifting and sorting. Other tools work well for digging.

40

STEM
Start

Hiding is a fun and special activity that some children love. When they are playing hide-and-seek, or just hiding in the natural areas, talk with them about what makes a "good" hiding spot. They hide behind small and large shrubs and human-made objects. Sometimes the colors of your clothing helps you to hide. Animals' fur and body coverings help them to hide because they blend in with their surroundings.

41

STEM
Start

Get to know a favorite tree on your school grounds. Provide tools and materials so that children can make representations of the tree through drawing, painting, sculpting, or digital photography. Name the parts of the tree and ask the children how they all work together as parts of the tree's "body." Visit the tree often and note seasonal changes. Try to depict the tree in different seasons and in different weather. How could you measure the tree? Provide tools, such as tape measures, yarn, or rope, to measure the circumference (distance around) of the tree.

42

Provide a variety of sticks for the children to line up by size, weight, and length. Sticks can be a very useful tool for counting, measuring, comparing, and sorting. Ask the children how they've sorted the sticks and which one is longest, shortest, or heaviest.

43

STEM
Start

Provide an assortment of sticks from different types of trees so the children can compare similarities and differences as well as note characteristics unique to one species or another. Practice observation skills by looking closely at the bark and the parts of a twig. Encourage the children to talk about what they see. Provide tools, such as magnifiers, paper, and pencils, for them to make observational drawings. The function of a twig is to support the leaves, which help the plant produce food through photosynthesis. It also contains tiny tubes that help it carry water and food to the tree.

44

STEM
Start

Collect seedpods from a variety of plants. Seeds are varied in their form, function, and structure. Encourage the children to sort and organize the seeds in a variety of ways. Talk about what you see and how the seeds might travel.

Seeds travel in a number of ways: on the air (wind), through animals' bodies (by being consumed and then excreted in feces or by clinging to fur), and by moving across the ground (such as rolling). How does their structure or shape help them move around? Provide tools for examining the seeds closely. See how you can move the seeds. Might seeds be carried on water?

45

STEM
Start

Life cycles can be investigated if you have a garden or can observe plants over time. What things change as the seasons change? Make a list of all the things you know will change over time and keep a daily log of what changes. You can also track the time that it takes for sprouts to emerge in the spring. This activity can help children understand that time is one way that we measure things.

46

STEM
Start

Take a series of time-lapse photos of plants or of one particular spot in your school yard. Combine the images after several weeks and watch them on a projector. This can help children get a sense of how things change over time. Change is often too slow for us to observe, so time-lapse photos help use see changes more readily.

47

STEM
Start

When children are digging in sand or soft mud, provide materials such as flat pieces of bark or sticks for them to use in bridge building. Encourage them to create a bridge that spans a moat or pond of their own creation. How can you create a bridge with these materials? What does your bridge need to be strong?

48
STEM
Start

When children move items across surfaces (for example, sliding sticks across the surface of a frozen puddle), point out how the motion of the items changes. Sometimes they go in a straight line; other times the direction curves or changes. Speculate about why this might be. Challenge them to try to make their sticks slide in a straight line. How far can you slide the sticks? Is there a way you could measure the distance? What tools could you use?

49
STEM
Start

Pay attention to the way things move, such as branches blowing in a breeze or leaves floating along the surface of a stream. Notice the way common animals, such as ducks or squirrels move. Talk together about what makes motion. (Motion is a movement from one place to another.) Identify examples of motion outdoors.

50
STEM
Start

While children are noticing and identifying motion, discuss what sorts of forces can cause motion. Any push or pull on something causes motion. For example, the wind is a push of air. A duck's paddling is a push and pull, resulting in the duck's forward motion. The children can push, pull, shove, or tug on objects to move them and also to move their bodies in space. All these words describe different forces. What forces can stop motion?

51

STEM Start

Provide materials to inspire the creation of rafts, boats, or other small objects that will float in the water. Talk with the children about the materials they select, as well as how they construct their objects. If an object sinks rather than floats, try to determine why. If an object floats, see how many loose parts, such as stones, pinecones, or leaves, it can support. Add additional items and encourage the children to make predictions about how many objects their raft will hold.

52

STEM Start

Listening for different sounds can become a habit when groups venture out of doors, and children can be challenged to compare sounds by pitch (low or high) or volume (loud or quiet). Ask them to identify similarities and differences in the sounds they hear. Some ideas include human-made sounds or sounds from nature. Do you hear different things at different times of day? Can you identify a rhythm or pattern in the sounds you hear?

53

STEM Start

Provide tubes, hoses, and funnels, and invite the children to make noises into them and tell you what they hear. Are the sounds different or the same? How does the sound change? Does it get louder? Provide different lengths and diameters of hoses and tubing so they can compare.

54
STEM
Start

Estimate the distance of lightning. (Note: When there is thunder or lightning, children should be indoors.) While watching through a window, wait for a flash of lightning. The lightning will usually be followed by a clap of thunder. Older children can calculate how far the lightning is by counting the time that elapses between seeing the lightning and hearing the thunder. Generally, each second of delay between the lightning and the thunder correlates to approximately one-fifth of a mile.

55
STEM
Start

Use natural objects to create musical instruments. Sticks can be rubbed or struck against one another, rocks can be rubbed together, dried seedpods can be shaken rhythmically. Experiment with different objects and create your own repeating rhythmic patterns. What are the best materials for making loud sounds? Quiet sounds? Patterns of sounds?

56
STEM
Start

Notice how light falls in different areas, such as through leaves and pine needles, creating shadows on the forest floor. How does light look when it's reflected off the surface of a lake or pond? What does the ground feel like when light is shining on it? Place a pile of rocks or sand in an area where the sunlight will shine on them for a few hours, and then enjoy the warm feeling. Compare to sand or stones that have been sitting in the shade. How might you measure the difference in temperature?

57
STEM Start

Feel and describe temperatures. Compare temperatures of water (either in shallow pans or a natural water feature, if you have one) and temperatures of stones and leaves. Put bare hands in the snow for a second or two to experience the freezing cold. What temperatures do the children prefer? Why?

58
STEM Start

Heat is a form of energy that is produced by motion. Have the children rub stones against flat pieces of wood, and then feel the wood. It will be warm to the touch due to friction. Have them rub their hands together to warm them. Heat is also produced by the sun. They can experience this by standing in the sun on a warm day.

59
STEM Start

If your site allows children to be near fires, compare materials for kindling. Which materials burn the best in a campfire? Why? What do you notice about the materials that burn? What happens if you put wet wood into a fire?

60
STEM Start

Paint with water on a sidewalk or large, flat boulder. The sun will evaporate the water (turn it to a gas), and it will fade away. Experiment with different locations and amounts of water, even different liquids.

61

STEM Start

Ribbons can be twirled, swirled, and waved through the air to learn about motion and wind. Provide an assortment of ribbons of various materials and invite the children to compare how they move in the wind.

62

STEM Start

Rain gauges are easy to make and use. Simply provide clear containers and permanent markers or another way to mark quantities on the outside of the container. Create a few rain gauges to place in different areas around the school yard.

63

STEM Start

Birdbaths will invite feathered friends to your site year-round. Many people make birdbaths out of simple shallow trays or pans set on stumps or on the ground. Experiment with different locations and observe where the birds prefer a bath. From a distance, observe how they bathe and drink. Look at the way that they use their beaks and wings for bathing and drinking. If you don't want to use a tray of standing water, rig up a mister hose in a tree and watch the birds (and children) visit frequently to cool off in the water spray.

64

STEM Start

Learn about insulative properties of materials by comparing the temperatures of dark fabric and light fabric. This can also be done with painted buckets filled with water and comparing the water temperatures. How could you design a very warm jacket? What color would it be?

65

STEM Start

Create levers by using flat pieces of wood on triangle blocks, and encourage the children to use the levers to lift things. Experiment with placing things at the ends of the lever, and learning how to balance them and move them for different results. Where can you find other examples of levers (crowbar, claw hammer)? Items like scissors, wire cutters, or pliers are made up of two levers.

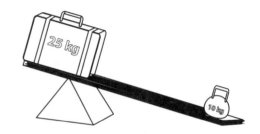

66

STEM Start

Wheels and axles are simple machines. Children can look closely at wheelbarrows, wagon wheels, and bike wheels to see how they work. Wheels help us move loads farther than a lever can. When do children use wheels and axles? How do wheelbarrows help you move heavy loads? Compare pulling materials in a sled or other flat-bottomed carrier to a wheelbarrow.

67
STEM Start

A wedge is a triangle. It works like a ramp, and it can help us split materials apart. Chisels, nails, knives, and saws are all examples of wedges. Trowels, spades, shovels, and many birds' beaks are wedges. They help split or break open materials. Try to find natural examples of wedges, such as chunks of rock or bark. How can you use them in your building or creating?

68
STEM Start

Invite the children to come up with code languages or ways to spread messages without speaking. Rock cairns (piles or stacks of rock), leaves arranged in distinct patterns, or sticks pointing like arrows are all ways that children might communicate without speaking. Come up with some code languages of your own.

69
STEM Start

Create flying things. Explore air and wind by making materials that fly or float on the wind. Kites can be fashioned out of leaves and twine or plastic bags and strings. Take the kites outside and experiment with running up and down hills, or with pulling them through the air to see how they move. Folded paper or cardboard can be turned into paper airplanes or other flying creations. What modifications need to be made to the objects to get them to fly farther? Better? Faster?

70

STEM
Start

Create measuring systems. To measure length, students might use sticks of uniform length, rope, or twine. To measure depth, they might use long poles or dowels. Provide a balance scale for them to measure weight. Liquids can be measured in thimbles, small and large cups, barrels, and bowls. Encourage them to create their own units of measurement and name them. There are many different ways that we measure things. Some are more accurate than others. There are times when it's important to be very accurate and times when it doesn't matter as much.

71

STEM
Start

Preserve leaves and flowers in a flower press. Use sheets of cardboard and pieces of paper. Layer the leaves on one piece of paper and stack another piece on top. Do this as many times as you like, then press a heavy board or bricks on top of the leaves. After a few days to a week, they will be flattened and dried and may be preserved under clear adhesive-backed paper or sealed with decoupage medium. This will enable you to examine them very closely, count leaves and petals, and look for patterns.

72

STEM
Start

Patterns in nature. Where can you find patterns? Pinecones, the arrangement of petals on a stem, seedheads, and the branching patterns of shells and leaves are all natural patterns. Look closely with magnifiers and other tools to identify spiraling patterns, hexagon patterns, and symmetry. Learn more about the Fibonacci sequence online and find Fibonacci numbers in natural materials.

73
STEM
Start

Spiders weave webs to catch insects to eat. While exploring outdoors, look for spiderwebs. Morning is the best time to do this, particularly if there is dew on the ground, which makes the webs more visible. Photograph or draw the webs that you see. Are they symmetrical? What is the pattern like? Where do spiders seem to prefer to make their webs?

74
STEM
Start

Use natural materials to build nests or other shelters similar to bird nests. Look online or in books for photographs of different types of nests. Children can try their hand at weaving, pressing, and fastening grasses and twigs together with mud.

75
STEM
Start

Create forts and hiding spots. Children love to have places that are just their size. They like to hide in them and also like a quiet place to call their own. Provide plenty of materials for building forts, including long branches, leaves, pine boughs, bamboo mats, and fabric pieces, and let children create forts of their own. They will experiment with different sizes and shapes of forts, finding and building forts that are just right. They'll be challenged to measure, estimate, and predict.

76

STEM Start

During any season, venture outdoors and collect interesting natural materials. Then call the children together to arrange them in patterns. Ask them to describe the patterns and the objects. What characteristics do the objects share? What makes them different? Identify textures, sizes, colors, shapes, living/nonliving.

77

STEM Start

If you have digital cameras or other picture-taking devices, encourage the children to document natural materials based on color, size, pattern, and scale. For example, they may take pictures of the clouds in the sky or wide-open spaces to illustrate "bigness," and they may take pictures of tiny mosses or seeds on the forest floor to illustrate "smallness."

78

STEM Start

If you live in a climate where water freezes in winter, fill pans or find puddles where children can measure the temperature of water and explore its properties. Then place the pans or other containers outside so they will freeze overnight. The next day, explore the ice and invite the children to describe it. How is it the same or different from liquid water? Provide salt for the children to put on the ice (it speeds the melting process) and ask them to describe their observations. Provide them with other materials, such as gravel and sand, and invite them to explore.

79
STEM Start

Collect a variety of small to medium-size rocks and stones. Work with the children to build towers out of the rocks. This will require balance and patience! Children will need to get to know the properties of the rocks to build and balance.

80
STEM Start

Provide a variety of child-sized rakes and other tools for moving leaves or other materials. Invite the children to create leaf mazes or trails of leaves for one another to follow. If you don't have leaves, you can do this with snow, sand, seaweed, gravel, and more. How long can the trails be? What works well for moving a lot of material? Can you make tunnels and piles as well as trails? Why or why not?

81
STEM Start

Use loose parts from nature, such as twigs, stones, seeds, and shells, to create patterns. Much like you'd do in the classroom with attribute blocks, invite children to create repeating patterns, alternating patterns, and patterns of their own design. Seek out patterns in natural materials, such as seed heads, pinecones, and flowers.

82

STEM Start

Observe shadows in different places. Notice what kinds of things create shadows and when. Provide paper and art materials and invite children to trace around the outer edge of shadows cast by leaves as they sit under trees.

83

STEM Start

Create a construction zone using plant materials. Children love to make small fairy houses or tiny homes for other creatures. Encourage them to do so on their own or with friends. Talk with children about their choices. How do different materials function in the homes? What sorts of materials are they selecting for different jobs? Why?

84

STEM Start

Create a space for gardening. Gardening offers children many affordances for STEM learning and engagement, Older children can measure, plan, and prepare digging sites, while younger ones may experiment with different tools for digging.

85

STEM Start

Provide seeds or bulbs for children to plant, and create ways to measure and monitor the seeds' growth. Some teachers encourage children to make observational drawings on a regular basis; others use photography as a form of documentation. Either way, be sure to find time to make regular visits so that the children can observe the emergence and growth of the seeds. Numerous citizen science projects involve tracking the growth of plants. See the resources in appendix A for ideas.

86

STEM Start

Provide garden tools, such as wheelbarrows, hand pumps, hoses, or watering cans, and ask the children to describe the different parts of the machines and tools they're using. How do the machines and tools make the work easier? What are the important components of the machines and tools? What would happen if some of those parts were missing or different? (For example, the nozzle on the hose or the wheel on the wheelbarrow.)

87

STEM Start

Extended periods of time outdoors means that your class will, at some point, likely encounter a dead bird or small mammal. This can present a unique and memorable opportunity for learning and investigating. If the animal's body is still relatively fresh and in good condition, provide gloves for any children who wish to touch it. Use the opportunity to get a close-up look at the feathers or fur of the animal, as well as its head, feet, and other body parts. Engage the children in discussions about what may have happened to the animal, and what (if anything) you should do with the body. Some children may wish to have a funeral for it, others may not. Some early childhood teachers who have encountered dead animals mark off the location and return for future visits so that the children can observe changes over time and learn more about what happens to the animal as it decomposes. They will be excited to learn more about how other animals feed on the body and how it helps create rich, fertile ground for plants to grow in as it decays.

88

STEM Start

Crayon rubbings are a very popular early childhood activity. Try doing rubbings of tree bark, rock textures, leaves, feathers that you find, and more. You may also wish to use waxed paper and a rock instead of a crayon for an entirely different type of image. Try making rubbings with different materials, observe and describe patterns, and compare and contrast the properties of each.

89

STEM Start

Lying on their bellies on the forest floor, children have an intimate view of the microworlds of insects and other arthropods, and plants. Many children love to watch and participate in these small worlds, and find the act of hunting for small creatures very exciting. Engage children in a discussion about size and scale. How do we measure sizes? When we say something is "small," what do we mean? Why is size an important characteristic to understand? Encourage children to draw or photograph small objects and animals, or to make models of them with art materials. How do they represent size?

90

STEM Start

Many children love ladybugs. During warm and sunny days, explore and look for ladybugs in your class garden. Encourage the children to search high and low, and count ladybugs in a small area. (Section off an area using ribbon or a hula hoop.) Invite the children to find objects that are comparable in size to a ladybug (such as pebbles or seeds) and use them as a measuring tool to estimate how many ladybugs might fit in a container, on a jar lid, under a leaf, or in other objects.

91

STEM Start

If you live in a region with snow in the winter, sledding can be a wonderful way to investigate engineering and physical science. Provide a lot of materials for the children to use for sleds, such as toboggans, sheets of paper, plastic, and fabric. Ask the children about how the different materials work as sleds. Which materials help them go fast? Which materials make them move more slowly? Does the shape of the sled make a difference? Are certain types of snow better for sledding?

92

STEM Start

Set up a tool station for children to do construction. Include real tools that are scaled for children's hands, such as coping saws, hammers, nails, screwdrivers, and wood glue. Allow them opportunities to create things out of wood, such as sundials, birdhouses or perches, shovels, rafts or boats. Children will have a lot of ideas about what they'd like to build. Provide close supervision and teach the children how to use the tools correctly.

93

STEM Start

Using mirrors to explore the natural world can be an exciting and intriguing change. Provide unbreakable mirrors for children to use to look more closely at things, explore symmetry, and use to reflect the sky or sunlight. (Be sure not to reflect light directly into anyone's eyes.) Mirrors can also provide a different perspective on landscapes and other natural features. Encourage the children to use the mirrors to explore and examine nature in whatever ways are interesting to them.

94

STEM Start

Provide a lot of art materials for children to draw or sketch animals and plants that they see outdoors. Encourage them to look closely at the attributes of the objects they are drawing. Drawing offers children the opportunity to attend to certain characteristics of objects, deciding what's important to include and what isn't. Ask them to describe their drawings and talk about what they included in their pictures. Encourage them to draw something they can return to again and again, such as a tree, and notice how their drawings change over time. What details are included? What's left out?

95
STEM Start

Look closely at a tree and describe what you see. What parts of the tree are hidden from view? What do the different parts of the tree do? Who lives in a tree? How do trees help animals?

96
STEM Start

Most children think of flowers when asked about plants. But plants are much more than flowers. Ask children what plants need to grow and what makes something a plant. If they don't know, invite them to show you all the different plants they can. Most children will recognize that plants grow out of the ground, have leaves and stems, and are usually green. Then discuss their common features. Compare them to objects that aren't plants, such as insects, stones, or other materials.

97
STEM Start

Drop paper confetti or flower petals in a puddle or pond and notice the way they move. Children can blow on them to move them across the water, make them spin, or gently drift along. This is a tangible way for children to experience air and the fact that air can move things.

98
STEM Start

Provide glass containers, such as bottles, to children and invite them to fill them with water at different levels. Then use sticks or wooden mallets to lightly strike the different bottles, noticing the different tones that are made. Encourage them to notice the connection between the level of water in the bottles with the tones created.

99
STEM Start

If you hear children express the sentiment that the plant or tree is "dead" (and you're sure it isn't), instead of verbally correcting their misconception, try engaging them in investigation. Invite them to come up with a list of characteristics of living plants. How do they know when a plant or tree is alive? (Some suggestions: they grow, they sprout leaves, the leaves are green, they may display flowers.) Create your list together and then develop a plan for how you can observe the tree over time to see if it exhibits any characteristics as the seasons change. This engages children in reflecting on what they know and referring to their prior knowledge about plants and trees (identifying characteristics they have seen in living trees) and in predicting what might happen to the tree you're studying over time. They will also practice observing as the tree changes in response to the temperature and amount of sunlight. You may also engage them in developing tools for measuring the plant or tree (such as a tape measure, counting links, rope, or other ways). It will be hard to see significant changes in tree growth, but herbaceous plants (plants without woody stems) will grow quickly, and their height can be measured and change observed over time.

100
STEM Start

If a child is digging in hard soil with a plastic shovel that breaks, he might select the next nearest tool to continue digging the hole. He reaches for a small rake but quickly becomes frustrated at having to use it to try to dig. He sets the rake aside and reaches for a large metal spoon, which is a better digging tool, but it makes the work go much more slowly.

By engaging this boy in a conversation about his tool selection, the teacher can learn more about what he knows about certain tools and why some work better than others. She can ask him what features of the shovel make it a good digging tool and why the rake is not so good for that purpose. She can elicit his understanding of the similarities between the spoon and the shovel and what makes them better tools than the rake for this job. She can ask him how he might make the job go faster even though the best tool to use is the spoon, which makes the job go much more slowly than the shovel did. In his responses, the boy will likely describe the soil he is trying to

move and how the texture of the soil factors into his decisions about tool selection. This demonstrates an awareness of the properties of soil, and the teacher can go one step further by asking him if he knows of any way he could change the soil to make it less hard.

This boy uses tools to move soil and mud from one place to another.

101
STEM Start

Children can look closely at tree bark and notice the number of colors or shapes present in the bark. They can look at leaves and count the points or lobes as part of their observation. (Bonus: This also helps them identify and count measurable attributes, an important math skill.)

102

Another way to practice the skill of observation is to place a few like natural objects, such as a few pinecones, in an opaque fabric bag or other container. Have children reach in and try to describe the objects they are feeling. The goal is *not* to name the object but to notice details and make observations about what they feel. It can be very challenging, especially for younger children, not to call out, "Pinecones!" as soon as they identify the object. Help them develop self-regulation by encouraging them to share their ideas about what the objects feel like instead of calling out the names of the objects. Encourage them to use words such as *cool* or *warm*, *hard* or *soft*, *bumpy* or *smooth*. This can be a fun and engaging game for children of all ages, and older children can be challenged not to repeat another word someone else has already used. You can also give them all their own "mystery bag" and invite them to draw the object inside just by gathering information about its size, shape, and texture through feeling the object. This is great for older children and provides an opportunity to use spatial thinking skills by rotating and visualizing the object and then representing it as a two-dimensional drawing.

103

Sit together in a circle outdoors. Have the children listen for sounds and hold up one finger for each sound they hear. While counting is an important skill in and of itself, this becomes a nice exercise in spatial awareness when children are also challenged to point in the direction from where the sounds originate.

104

STEM Start

Changing temperatures outdoors present a great opportunity for children to learn about heat loss and insulation. The human body is constantly trying to maintain a regular temperature and gains and loses heat all the time, mostly through the head, hands, and feet (this is why warm socks, mittens, and hats are so important!). We generate body heat mostly through physical activity. Clothing layers such as hats or wool mittens themselves do not "make you warmer"—they keep your body warm by preventing heat loss. Some materials and fabrics are much better at this than others. Can you think of any examples?

105

STEM Start

As scary as bees and wasps may be for young children, insect encounters present many STEM teaching opportunities. You might notice a child's fear and let that lead to an investigation about the role of these insects in nature, such as for pollinating plants or serving as food sources for other animals. You might take the opportunity to look closely at the insects (if the child is comfortable or willing to give it a try) to learn more about their bodies and the way they work.

106
STEM
Start

Do you have a post-and-platform play structure? If so, even that can provide some opportunities for STEM investigations. For example, notice how the children experiment with balance and center of gravity as they play on a teeter-totter. A playground slide provides opportunities to experiment with an inclined plane or ramp. And if you are lucky enough to have sand in your play area, you have plenty of opportunities for STEM learning. Sand offers an invitation to dig, pile, tunnel, and push it around. Children love to scoop and carry sand. They can be mesmerized by its softness, its coolness and warmth, and the different sizes of sand grains. Children drag sticks across sand and create patterns and designs, experimenting with aesthetics. They vary the amount of pressure on the stick to create new patterns, and in doing so, they learn about tool use and the properties of sand and other materials, such as sticks, leaves, pine needles, and stones. They dig deep holes and discover the damp layers of sand hidden beneath. They look for opportunities to move it from place to place. Sand on the surface of a slide or platform changes its texture completely, offering new sensory input and varying the physical challenge of walking or moving on that surface.

107
STEM
Start

Make puppets out of leaves, grasses, and other materials you find outdoors. Children can create their own puppet shows for one another. They may be inspired to make characters of all shapes, sizes, and personalities. They may even make homes or towns for their puppets. Children demonstrate their knowledge about animals' needs, behavior, and lives when they engage in dramatic play, such as puppetry involving animals.

108
STEM
Start

Create music together out of instruments you build or sounds you create by rubbing stones together, banging sticks, shaking seedpods, or swishing bundles of grasses. Invite the children to make up rhythms and patterns out of sound.

109
STEM
Start

Provide ropes and cords (with adult supervision, of course) and encourage children to tie them to various objects, then push, pull, lift, and haul. You may introduce a pulley so that children can experiment with how it helps them move heavy objects.

110
STEM
Start

String cords from branch to branch and hang things from them, such as baskets, ribbons, or even wind chimes. Watch how different objects affect the cords and branches. Experiment with different placements to harness more or less wind.

111
STEM
Start

Weave grasses, flower stems, and leaves into ropes, crowns, belts, or just pretty "charms." See what materials work well for weaving and how you can weave long, wide, strong, or fluttery things.

112
STEM
Start

Invite each child to create a "smell jar." Provide small glass or plastic containers and encourage the children to find items outdoors that have interesting smells (for example, dried sage, pine needles, wet leaves, flower petals). They can mix different materials together or use one jar for each item. They will enjoy trying to "stump the teacher" if you try to guess the contents of each jar.

113
STEM
Start

Build fences and borders out of twigs tied together with grasses or ribbon. You may create lines of stones, dig shallow trenches, or create long, narrow piles of leaves to mark borders and patterns together. Borders and fences made of footprints in the sand or snow are also fun to create. Children love to create spaces for themselves, "roads," " trails," or pathways.

114
STEM
Start

Create miniature gardens by arranging small stones, bits of moss, flower petals, sand, and soil in pie plates or other containers. Children enjoy creating "small worlds" for fairies or other imaginary creatures.

115
STEM Start

Carve wood or whittle branches. If children are too young to use sharp tools, provide spoons or jagged stones. (Make sure the wood is rotten so it will be soft enough to carve in this way.) Children can rub the ends of branches against stones to sharpen them.

116
STEM Start

Place a bundle of bells on the ground and have one child sit near them with eyes closed (or a scarf over the eyes if the child is comfortable). Other children try to creep quietly up and snatch the bells. If the child with eyes closed hears a sound, she points in the direction of the sound before the "creeper" can grab the bells.

117
STEM Start

Invite the children to invent a treasure hunt that relates to some theme. For example, find five things with a pattern in nature, or find five things that start with the letter *s*. The possibilities of this type of treasure hunt are endless.

118
STEM Start

Try measuring the "biggest." Head out in search of the biggest boulder, tree, dirt pile, etc. Invite the children to measure it with their bodies. How many kids holding hands will it take to go around the tree trunk? This game also works with the "smallest," the "longest," and so forth.

119

STEM
Start

Invite the children to create obstacle courses out of twigs, bricks, sand piles, logs, etc., and move through the obstacle courses in different ways (on your belly, hopping on one foot, etc.).

120

STEM
Start

Bring a variety of natural objects such as logs, rocks, pumpkins, watermelons, etc., to a small hill and experiment with rolling the objects down the hill.

121

STEM
Start

Create piles of leaves or branches and invite children to throw lightweight balls at the piles to experiment with how hard to throw to knock them down, practice aiming, etc.

122

STEM
Start

Create mudballs and throw them at a sheet or large piece of cardboard. Children will love the opportunity to see the mud splatter and will enjoy experimenting to find just the right consistency of mud to get the desired effect.

Appendix A: Resources for Increasing Your STEM Understanding

Access the full list of the Next Generation Science Standards and the "crosscutting concepts" at these websites. There, you can learn more about the standards—and even sort by discipline, grade level, thinking practices, and more.

Next Generation Science Standards: www.nextgenscience.org

Crosscutting concepts: www.nextgenscience.org/sites/default/files /Appendix%20G%20-%20Crosscutting%20Concepts%20FINAL%20 edited%204.10.13.pdf

Children and Nature Network aims to connect all children, their families and communities to nature through innovative ideas, evidence-based resources and tools, broad-based collaboration and support of grassroots leadership. Learn more at www.childrenandnature.org.

Common Sense Media is the leading independent nonprofit organization dedicated to helping children thrive in a world of media and technology. They empower parents, teachers, and policy makers by providing unbiased information, trusted advice, and innovative tools to help them harness the power of media and technology as a positive force in all chilren's lives. Learn more at www.commonsensemedia.org.

The International Technology and Engineering Educators Association (ITEEA) is the professional organization for technology, innovation, design, and engineering educators. Their mission is to promote technological literacy for all by supporting the teaching of technology and engineering and promoting the professionalism of those engaged in these pursuits. ITEEA strengthens the profession through leadership, professional development, membership services, publications, and classroom activities. Learn more at www.iteea.org.

The National Aeronautics and Space Administration has a wealth of educational resources for children and for educators, particularly related to earth and space science. Learn more at www.nasa.org.

National Association for the Education of Young Children hosts an early childhood science interest forum and a young children and nature interest forum. Both seek to connect practitioners with resources and networking opportunities. NAEYC also offers a good selection of materials related to inclusion, diversity, and anti-bias curriculum. Learn more at www.naeyc.org.

National Association for the Education of Young Children (NAEYC) and National Council of Teachers of Mathematics (NCTM) position paper "Where Do We Stand on Early Childhood Mathematics" can be found at www.nctm.org/uploadedFiles/Standards_and_Positions/Position_Statements /Early%20Childhood%20Mathematics%20(2013).pdf.

National Science Teachers Association members have access to a lot of materials, including lesson plans, resource reviews, and articles specifically aimed at early childhood educators. Please see the NSTA/NAEYC joint position statement on early childhood science education which can be downladed at www.nsta.org /about/positions/earlychildhood.aspx.

The Natural Start Alliance is a coalition of educators, parents, organizations, and others who want to help young children connect with nature and care for the environment. Natural Start is a project of the North American Association for Environmental Education. Natural Start connects the people who teach young children—whether they are professionals or parents—with the tools they need to create great educational experiences that help young children explore the natural world, understand their environment, and build lifelong skills that will help them stay active and engaged in their communities. Learn more at www.naturalstart.org.

The National Council of Teachers of Mathematics is the public voice of mathematics education, supporting teachers to ensure equitable mathematics learning of the highest quality for each and every student through vision, leadership, professional development, and research. Learn more at www.nctm.org.

North American Association for Environmental Education (NAAEE) brings the brightest minds together to advance environmental literacy and civic engagement through the power of education to create a more sustainable future for all. Visit their website to learn more about environmental education and download their Guidelines for Effective Early Childhood Environmental Education at https://naaee.org/sites/default/files/final_ecee _guidelines_from_chromographics_lo_res.pdf.

Office of Head Start Inclusion Resources exists to increase the competence, confidence, and effectiveness of personnel in Head Start programs to include children with disabilities. Their website has training materials, tools for teachers and coordinators, as well as other resources. Learn more at www .headstartinclusion.org.

"Proper Use of Playback in Birding." If, like many teachers, you wish to use recordings of birds to aid in your birdfinding investigations, please review the following guidelines first to ensure ethical treatment of birds and other animals www.sibleyguides.com/2011/04/the-proper-use-of-playback-in-birding.

The Stop Faking It series from NSTA Press provides a good overview of basic science concepts, including air and weather, light, and electricity. Learn more at www.nsta.org/publications/press.

SciMathMN is a collaborative network of STEM education organizations based in Minnesota. Their website is full of information, including connections to national standards, and contains numerous resources for educators located anywhere. Learn more at scimathmn.org.

www.teachengineering.org is a website with K–12 engineering curricula, lesson plans, resources, and information about engineering.

Appendix B: Taking STEM Outside

THESE CHARTS WILL HELP YOU IDENTIFY children's engagement in the practices of STEM in nature-based contexts. It also lists specific things to watch for and ways you can support STEM engagement in nature play.

Science and Engineering Practices

Science and engineering practices	What young children do	What this looks like outdoors
Ask questions	Notice, wonder, and raise questions about the environment or materials	Look at and inspect objects in the natural world Listen to different sounds, comment on things they see or wonder about Use a variety of senses to explore the natural world Experiment with their bodies (i.e., climbing, moving heavy things, stacking objects—asking themselves "What can I do?")
Identify problems	Recognize that there are things that need to be fixed or created	Build things and design solutions to solve problems in play Discuss solutions to problems or ideas about what might make something work better "Tinker" with materials and objects to understand their properties and discover how they work together. Construct fairy houses, homes or "caves" for themselves or other creatures Build bridges, forts, other shelters

Develop and use models	Make representations (through drawing, painting, dramatic play)	Engage in play about being animals
		Create miniature structures such as homes, towns, and cities for animals out of toys or loose parts
		Use loose parts to represent animals or characters or other "props" in play
		Use objects and materials to represent systems or processes (i.e., water from a sprinkling can is "rain")
Plan and carry out investigations	Generate new ideas for exploration or just go and do	Investigate phenomena through trial and error, repeated encounters with material, trying new things, attempting to use materials in new ways
		Asking questions like "What will happen if . . ." Or "How can I make X happen?"
		Investigate force and motion, cause and effect.
		Engage in fearless or tentative exploration of environment
Analyze and interpret data	Think about, describe and discuss observations, understanding, and experience	Process experiences verbally, share observations with others
		Identify and predict seasonal changes and other natural phenomena
		Recognize a need to gather information in order to understand natural phenomena
		Discuss and describe what they see and do in nature
		Recognize and describe similarities, differences, evidence, and reasoning
Use mathematics and computational thinking	Talk about shapes, numbers, or count Recognize patterns Use mathematical language, such as *over*, *under*, *around*, and *through*	Count objects, animals, or materials.
		Use mathematical language when describing living and nonliving things.
		Use natural objects such as sticks to measure (distance, depth, size of objects)
		Seriate, identify, and compare attributes of objects; order and group objects into sets
		Create patterns with objects and materials
		Describe relationships between and among materials, objects, places, and phenomena in the natural world
		Describe and discuss scale, size, or distance when talking about natural places or materials

Construct explanations	Share ideas about why and how things happen	Explain natural phenomena to peers or adults
Design solutions (engineering)	Generate ideas about how to solve problems or meet needs	Create structures, rafts, platforms, and enclosures Create systems that are interconnected, such as pathways for moving water or natural objects or other materials Create tools out of natural materials Identify ways to improve structures, systems, or other creations
Engage in argument from evidence	Recognize and articulate observations and data Identify attributes Base predictions and understanding on previous experience or prior knowledge	Express reasoning to others, compare ideas and observations with those of others Explain ideas, make predictions, and draw conclusions about weather, animal behavior, seasonal changes, and other natural phenomena based on previous experience or prior knowledge
Obtain, evaluate, and communicate information	Document and share information Answer questions Share ideas and talk about investigations	Identify ways to learn about phenomena or materials; think about and share understanding. Compare objects, structures and systems, and living things, and articulate similarities and differences Identify systems and parts of systems and how they work (for example, articulate that a tree has distinct parts, such as roots, a trunk, branches, and leaves)

Technology Practices

Practices associated with technology and tools	What young children do	How to support this practice in nature-based settings
Questioning	Ask questions and express interest in tools, including their purpose and function Indicate interest in media and the subjects of media Recognize that media images of animals may differ from real animals	Provide lots of variety in tools and age-appropriate media related to the natural world. Be sure that a variety of races, genders, and abilities are presented. Critically examine portrayals of nature and animals in media. Discuss technology applications that are appropriate for a given purpose (for example, digital cameras). Provide a variety of tools to support children's investigations. Provide opportunities to use technology to help with knowledge construction.
Decision making	Select or create tools based on an identified need Make decisions about which media or technology will be most appropriate for a given task, be it investigation or communication Choose a form and means of communication	Provide a variety of tools and ensure that children know how to access and use them. Ask children how they would like to document or keep a record of their investigations or questions. Allow children access to plenty of different kinds of media and materials with which to represent their ideas and understanding.
Integration	Recognize that certain elements of designs and products have a function as well Use, request, or refer to available tools or technology with little or no prompting	Discuss the features of certain tools that make them well suited to a particular task; for example, consider a net with large holes compared to a fine mesh: which is better for catching insects?

Communication, expression, and representation	Use technology to enhance learning or record information	Provide digital cameras and audio recorders for children to document natural objects, systems, and processes in ways that are meaningful to them.
		Use bird and flower identification apps, field guides, pictures, and other materials to help them build knowledge of species names.
		Use videos or websites to see time-lapse photos or movies of natural phenomena, maps, and other things that would be difficult or impossible to see otherwise.

Mathematics Practices

Practices associated with mathematics	What young children do	How to support this outdoors
Problem solving	Formulate ideas, challenge their own thinking, describe their reasoning	Provide opportunities for fort building, collaborative work, and engineering "challenges." Allow time for them to deeply engage in projects or dramatic play. Ask them to describe their process to you.
		Say "I knew you could do it."
Reasoning	Identify patterns, discrepancies, and similarities, and make predictions based on prior knowledge	Engage them in conversations about decision and process.
		Provide lots of "loose parts" for building, arranging, manipulating.
	Synthesize information	Ask: "How are these the same? How are they different? How did you decide to do that? How did you know to do that? What happened when you...?" "What will happen if you...?"
Connecting and communicating	Develop understanding of relationships between and among objects and phenomena, including cause and effect	Ask children to describe their thoughts, process, and understanding.
		Ask them to describe their observations and patterns they have seen.
	Share ideas and findings with others	Ask groups of children to describe how they built something together (such as a bridge or a fort).

Representing	Use pictures, diagrams, or objects to represent a situation or idea	Provide loose parts for play. Ask children to represent their thinking in drawings, sketches, or 3D creations using loose parts.

Supporting Big Ideas through Nature Play

Included is a list of provocations or entry points for children to engage in these big ideas, followed by specific ways you can support this behavior outdoors through prompts, play affordances, or materials and landscape elements.

Big ideas specific to science	What young children notice or respond to	What you can do to support this curiosity outdoors	Natural materials and landscape elements to include; recommended tools for exploration
Living things and life cycles	Express interest in living things and being near living things Show compassion and concern when living things are injured or dying Ask questions like "Is this real?" Structure and shape of animals, plants, insects	Look for opportunities for children to engage with animals, plants, trees, or other living things. Notice when children identify structures or "parts of a whole." Be aware of structure and function in organisms such as plants and animals (for example, the parts of insects or the parts of trees).	Plants and plant materials Logs or leaf litter under which to look for arthropods Tools (nets, jars, sheets) and instruction for carefully collecting small creatures for temporary observation Cultivated gardens where children can grow edible plants and plants that can be examined and used for loose part play Variety of textures, materials of plants Sticks, "tree cookies," and leaves; tree stumps or fallen logs for climbing Dense shrubs for children to play around and hide behind Explore structures of organisms (for example, tree roots, trunk, branches, leaves)

The earth and space	Notice and wonder about the sun, moon, and stars Talk about planet Earth Recognize pictures of planet Earth	Provide opportunities to investigate soils, landforms, the sun, sky, stars, water, rocks, seasonal changes. Talk about the role of earth in space. Encourage families to do skywatching and moon gazing. Provide opportunities to be outdoors at a variety of times, including early morning and evening, if possible, when moon and/or stars may be visible.	Mud, dirt, sand, stones Variation in terrain (such as small hills, valleys) Variety of earth materials, such as small and large stones, some big enough for climbing Water access, such as a hose or hand pump, or small moving water, such as a shallow creek or stream Binoculars, shovels, trowels, sieves for sorting sand and gravel; wheelbarrows for moving large amounts of earth
Materials, structure and function of materials	Explore materials through digging, scooping, shoveling, pouring, and full-body immersion Notice and talk about shapes and structures of objects, including human-made structures and materials (school buildings, sidewalks) Ask questions about the function of certain objects Use tools strategically Use of simple machines to assist in work Identify parts that make up a system, for example, parts of a tree or streams that flow into a lake	Allow children to use all their senses to explore earth materials. Ask children about different characteristics of objects, such as plants, rocks, insects, and other natural features that have interesting structures. Provide hand lenses for exploring structures. Offer natural materials and structures with different textures, such as wood, mud, clay, stones, or sticks. Use different materials for strategic purposes (such as tinkering and constructing). Talk together about the function of natural and human-made objects. Explore how simple machines work.	Sand, mud, dirt areas for digging and exploring properties of earth materials Provide shovels, scoops, and containers in and around mud and shallow water features Tools such as shovels, funnels, sieves, nets, containers of various sizes and types, hand lenses Variety of natural materials with interesting structures: vines, woody plants, and herbaceous plants Access to trees, access to water so children can explore materials when wet Freedom and time to use materials in ways that let them explore properties Examples of simple machines, wood or blocks cut into wedge shapes, ramps, inclined planes, sections of rain gutter, wood, or playground slide

Materials, structure and function of materials continued on next page.

	Recognize that when one part of a system is affected, the whole system is affected (such as removing a block from a structure, causing the whole structure to fail)	Provide loose parts and opportunities to investigate systems.	Screws for woodworking Levers, such as hammers or pry bars Pulleys hung from trees or over branches to help children transfer weight and lift objects Wheeled objects, such as wheelbarrows, for transporting materials Create systems for moving materials (sand, water, etc) with natural and human-made objects
Air and weather	Wind, rain, temperature changes Seasonal changes, wind, snow, drought	Spend time outdoors in all seasons and all weather (safety permitting). Encourage children to represent different weather through body movements, art, writing, and drawing. Spend time outdoors in all types of weather. Remark on and discuss weather and temperature. Offer children a variety of places to experience temperature changes, such as in the sun and shade or in covered shelters from the rain where they can still see, hear, and smell it.	Rain gauges, umbrellas, thermometers, anemometers, ribbons Trees so children may observe the effects of wind Sundial Create kites or other mechanisms that will respond to wind. Provide ribbons and lightweight materials that children can use to explore air and weather. Use technology to record data about seasonal changes, bloom times, etc. Participate in citizen science initiatives.

Forces and motion	Throwing rocks and sticks	Provide open spaces for running and throwing.	Slopes, ramps, materials that can be used to set things in motion
	Movement across different surfaces	Provide safe objects for throwing.	Hills, water features, or materials for moving water, such as hand pumps, water wheels, and things that pour
	Use of materials as tools to apply force or motion	Encourage them to move across different surfaces, such as sand, ice, concrete, snow, grass, etc.	Flexible plastic tubing for moving marbles or other small objects from place to place
	Constructing		Variety of natural surfaces where children can experiment with moving different objects, including simple machines
Energy and matter	Interest in solids, liquids, and gases	Provide opportunity to explore many solids and liquids.	Snow, water, mud, ice, dirt, rocks, etc., water access
		Notice the temperature changes.	Materials for changing the consistency and states of matter (e.g., water to add to dirt)
			Thermometers for measuring temperature

Supporting Big Ideas Specific to Math

Big ideas specific to math	What this looks like	What this looks like outside	How you can support this; tools and natural elements
Quantifying and counting	Counting, use of number names, awareness of cardinality (the last number counted is the total number of something)	Children may count loose parts and distribute materials among friends. Use of number names to represent a quantity of something	Allow lots of variety and loose parts for dramatic play. Ask children how many there are. Encourage their use of numbers. Provide a variety of containers for sorting and organizing materials.
Comparing	Direct matching of sets or demonstrating awareness of differences among sets or objects	"The rocks in this pile are bigger and heavier than the rocks in that pile." "That bird is blue, but the other one is gray."	Ask, "How are [these] like [those]? How are they different? How do these [sets, objects] compare?" Ask, "Is it warmer or cooler today than it was yesterday?" (Ask children to reflect on previous experience and compare.) Provide many loose parts Expose children to a diversity of plant and tree species. Show children boulders or large stones with visible differences and similarities. Obtain a balance scale that can be left outside. Provide chalk for tracing around objects or drawing representations of objects.

| Geometry and measurement | Determining the size, shape, and space of objects

Determining sizes, lengths, quantities or quantifying their attributes | Describing natural materials with words like *big, small, little, huge, round, square, tall, short, face, edge, side, surface, corner, angle*, etc.

Moving objects (or one's body) through space helps children learn about shape and space.

Describing length, distance, quantity, etc., of spaces or objects. Children may use "standard" measurement units or may develop their own ("This rock is three grasshoppers high"). | Ask children to describe things to you.

Encourage use of describing words. Ask children to imagine moving things: "Will this apple fit in my pocket?"

Provide tape measures, yardsticks, and other materials for measuring, including loose parts such as ribbons or strings.

Provide sticks so children may measure, compare, use for distance.

Feature pathways and wide-open areas.

Create enclosed spaces such as willow huts or forts.

Provide containers for moving and carrying water, sand, and other materials.

Allow lots of space to roam and run freely; provide obstacles and elements that require children to move over under, around, and through things.

Talk about length, distance, quantity, etc. Ask children to estimate distances and sizes. |

Materials That Support STEM in Outdoor Settings

Domain–specific content objectives (skills)	What young children will do in their nature play	Materials that help
Science	Observe closely Note attributes of materials Ask questions Demonstrate awareness of where things can be found in nature Demonstrate understanding of animal behavior (through play, representation, discussion) Identify characteristics of living things Identify where things live Identify what living things need Recognize and describe properties of objects and materials	Magnifiers such as hand lenses or binoculars Field guides or pictures Bird blinds (hiding places from which children can watch birds and other animals) Sandy surfaces or muddy areas where animal tracks can be observed Diversity of plants, rocks, other materials Art materials for journaling
Technology	Identify, choose, and describe tools for specific purposes Create tools or symbols to serve a purpose Use tools to explore the environment, such as shovels, trowels, measuring cups and spoons, funnels, pans, and other human-made tools. Use natural objects in place of human-made objects, such as bark and sticks for rafts or boats, stones for digging Use sticks for stacking, writing, poking, or stirring Use bowls or natural-made containers to transport water and other materials	Digital or other cameras, recording devices, flashlights, microscopes, mirrors, and all other tools mentioned on this chart

Engineering	Test their own strength and the strength of materials and explore balance through manipulation of materials Source materials Design under constraint Stack Create ramps Create tunnels Create piles Create walls Create tall structures Create long structures Create containers Support one thing with another Solve problems Create systems made up of parts	Blocks, sticks, bricks Large loose parts, small loose parts Simple machines Sections of gutter or PVC pipe, wood ramps and blocks that may be left outdoors Flat pieces of bark or logs, pinecones Small stones, sand String and yarn Flat surfaces for building Plastic-coated wires, large and small sticks for fort building and smaller creations Water and things with which to move water, such as tubes or gutters or hoses Earth-moving materials, such as shovels, trowels, wheelbarrow, etc. Woodworking equipment Freedom to manipulate environment Wide-open spaces to create large and/or complex systems Time to immerse in construction and to redesign
Math	patterning grouping sorting organizing (establish groups or sets) classifying (name sets or groups) seriating (line up by size) measuring use language and space to demonstrate awareness of over, under, around, and through emptying filling estimating measuring making maps create representations (3D models, drawings, dramatic play, etc.)	Loose parts: rocks, sticks, etc. Balance scale Measuring tools Different lengths of string, yarn, twine, and rope Hand lenses and "box magnifiers" Materials for drawing and making representations (chalk, paint, clay, etc.) Variety of containers for measuring, some with numbers or other units, others without Containers that will hold material such as water or sand, and other containers that have holes or slots Wheelbarrows for transporting and moving materials Open spaces, platforms, and white sheets for children to create patterns or representations Paper or art materials for making maps

Appendix C: Standards, Recommendations, and Guidelines

Much of the work I do as an educator is informed by the North American Association for Environmental Education's *Guidelines for Excellence in Early Childhood Programs*, a great resource for anyone wishing to incorporate more nature-based play and learning in their early childhood setting. These guidelines offer practical suggestions for planning early childhood curricula and programs that appeal to children's innate love and curiosity for the natural world. They are a rich resource for identifying features of a natural play setting, nature-based preschool, or nature-friendly primary setting, as well as for offering considerations for staff preparation and development, and community partnerships. The guidelines also offer practical suggestions for everything from accommodations for children with physical disabilities to safety and risk to culturally relevant approaches. They even provide helpful examples of interdisciplinary environmental activities. Check appendix A for the website where you can download a copy of the guidelines.

A note about standards: Many states have established academic standards or progress indicators for preschool-aged children in the areas of math and science. Early learning advocacy and service organizations, such as the National Association for the Education of Young Children and Head Start, have also established criteria that indicate high-quality programs. Many of those criteria include content-specific standards or benchmarks. Be sure to know what standards and guidelines apply to your individual setting.

Primary-grades educators have additional standards to consider. In 2013 the Next Generation Science Standards (NGSS) were developed to help educators engage students in science and engineering practices, while deepening their understanding of the core ideas and interrelationships in these fields. These standards affect the way science concepts and practices are taught, and they aim to identify *crosscutting concepts* (mentioned in chapter 6) that teachers should know—that is, ideas and themes that link ideas and practices across grade levels. The NGSS span grades K–12, but they contain core ideas that are relevant in the early childhood setting. While not every state has adopted the NGSS, these standards outline numerous process skills as well as ideas and concepts important in the disciplines of science and engineering that educators should consider. Moreover, since the early years are the time in which children are fully engaged in so many of the process skills of science, mathematics, and engineering, it is helpful to recognize how those skills progress and develop naturally as children age. The NGSS help to put a framework around that developmental progression. Pages 185–89 provide a list of the NGSS for K–2 and also include a link where you can download a full copy of the NGSS online.

The Common Core State Standards for Math (CCSS-M) impact the landscape of math education as well. Currently, forty-two states have adopted the CCSS-M. While the standards are aimed at K–12, they have led to much examination and discussion about math in the context of early childhood.

The National Council of Teachers of Mathematics (NCTM) has also established recommendations for teachers of young children as they relate to the CCSS-M. Along with the NAEYC, the NCTM has a position statement (link found in appendix A), which, among other things, encourages teachers of young children to "provide ample time, materials, and teacher support for children to engage in play, a context in which they explore and manipulate mathematical ideas with keen interest."

The intent of this book is not to suggest or imply that you link your explorations and curriculum to standards (although if you need or desire to do so, hopefully you will find resources here to help you); the goal is simply to make you aware of the array of academic, behavioral, and content standards that have an impact on how STEM subjects are taught and presented, and what some of the important process skills are that are associated with those disciplines. In some cases, it's helpful to think of standards in terms of how they might help you in scaffolding the work you do with children. For example, if you know that in your state, kindergarten students will be expected to demonstrate the skill of counting to twenty-five, it makes sense to provide lots of nature-based opportunities that you know will strengthen their mathematical understanding, so that they will later be successful in doing so.

No set of standards adequately addresses the social, emotional, and other needs of young children, particularly standards developed for and aimed at older children. Educators' continued commitment to developmentally appropriate practice, culturally relevant pedagogy, and a focus on the whole child is imperative. Standards are simply one piece of a greater set of tools that educators can refer to, when appropriate, in the interest of serving young children's needs.

According to the National Association for the Education of Young Children, there are "four conditions under which early learning standards should be developed and implemented" (NAEYC 2012, 5). While the conditions stated below come from the NAEYC's position paper on Common Core State Standards, they are appropriate for educators to consider when evaluating any set of guidelines or standards.

1. Early learning standards should emphasize significant developmentally appropriate content and outcomes.

2. Early learning standards are developed and reviewed through informed, inclusive processes.

3. Early learning standards gain their effectiveness through implementation and assessment practices that support children's development in ethical, appropriate ways.

4. Early learning standards require a foundation of support for early childhood programs, professionals, and families. (NAEYC 2012)

Essentially, any standards that are applied to young learners should be responsive to the unique needs of those young learners—everything from the way they are implemented to the way they are assessed and evaluated, and the way that those who are expected to implement them are supported by the larger community.

Appendix D: Chart of Crosscutting Concepts

The following chart provides you with links between the STEM starts and the crosscutting concepts, described on pages 119–21 (NGSS 2013).

To connect the STEM starts to the crosscutting concepts, be sure to think about the definition of crosscutting concepts (see page 119) and how you can use language, questions, tools, or other ways of engaging children in making the connections. Listen for their words and watch their actions to help you see evidence of awareness of the crosscutting concepts.

STEM START	Patterns	Cause and Effect	Scale, Proportion, and Quantity	Systems and System Models	Energy and Matter	Structure and Function	Stability and Change
1	X					X	
2	X					X	
3							X
4		X					
5		X				X	
6						X	
7						X	
8						X	
9			X				
10						X	
11			X				

STEM START	Patterns	Cause and Effect	Scale, Proportion, and Quantity	Systems and System Models	Energy and Matter	Structure and Function	Stability and Change
12	X					X	
13						X	X
14	X		X				X
15		X				X	
16		X				X	X
17			X			X	
18		X					
19						X	
20			X				
21		X					X
22		X					X
23		X			X		X
24		X		X			X
25	X		X				
26	X					X	
27						X	
28			X				
29		X			X		X
30		X			X	X	X
31				X			
32		X		X			X
33		X		X			
34		X					X
35			X			X	
36				X		X	
37		X					
38		X		X			
39						X	
40			X				
41						X	
42			X				

STEM START	Patterns	Cause and Effect	Scale, Proportion, and Quantity	Systems and System Models	Energy and Matter	Structure and Function	Stability and Change
43			X	X		X	
44	X					X	
45		X					X
46							X
47						X	
48		X					
49		X					
50		X					
51			X			X	
52		X					
53		X					
54		X					X
55		X				X	
56	X	X					X
57		X			X		X
58					X	X	
59					X	X	
60		X					X
61		X					
62			X				
63		X					
64						X	
65		X				X	
66		X				X	
67						X	
68	X						
69		X					
70			X				
71	X		X				
72	X					X	
73	X					X	

STEM START	Patterns	Cause and Effect	Scale, Proportion, and Quantity	Systems and System Models	Energy and Matter	Structure and Function	Stability and Change
74			X			X	
75			X			X	
76			X				
77			X				
78		X					
79		X				X	
80			X			X	
81	X						X
82		X					
83				X		X	
84							X
85		X					X
86		X				X	
87		X					X
88	X						
89			X				
90			X				
91						X	
92		X				X	
93	X					X	
94	X		X				
95				X			
96						X	
97		X			X		
98		X					
99		X					
100						X	
101						X	
102						X	
103		X					
104		X			X		

STEM START	Patterns	Cause and Effect	Scale, Proportion, and Quantity	Systems and System Models	Energy and Matter	Structure and Function	Stability and Change
105		X					
106					X	X	
107			X			X	
108	X					X	
109	X						
110	X					X	
111						X	
112						X	
113			X				
114			X				
115							X
116		X					
117	X					X	
118			X				
119			X	X			
120		X					
121		X					
122		X					

References

American Academy of Pediatrics. 2013. "The Crucial Role of Recess in School." *Pediatrics* 131 (1). http://pediatrics.aapublications.org/content/131/1/183.

Archer, L., J. DeWitt, J. Osborne, J. Dillon, B. Willis, and B. Wong. 2010. "'Doing' Science versus 'Being' a Scientist: Examining 10/11-year-old Schoolchildren's Constructions of Science through the Lens of Identity." *Science Education* 94 (4): 617–39.

Bandura, Albert. 2001. "Social Cognitive Theory: An Agentic Perspective." *Annual Review of Psychology* 52 (1): 1–26.

Baroody, Arthur J., Yingying Feil, and Amanda R. Johnson. 2007. "An Alternative Reconceptualization of Procedural and Conceptual Knowledge." *Journal for Research in Mathematics Education* 38 (2): 115–31.

Berger, R., and M. Lahad. 2010. "A Safe Place: Ways in Which Nature, Play and Creativity Can Help Children Cope with Stress and Crisis—Establishing the Kindergarten as a Safe Haven Where Children Can Develop Resiliency." *Early Child Development and Care* 180 (7): 889–900.

Biggs, Alton, and Patrick Tap. 1986. "The School Surroundings: A Useful Tool in Education." *American Biology Teacher* 48 (1): 27–31. doi:10.2307/4448182.

Centers for Disease Control and Prevention. 2013. *Voluntary Guidelines for Managing Food Allergies in Schools and Early Care and Education Programs*. Washington, DC: US Department of Health and Human Services. www.cdc.gov/healthyschools/foodallergies/pdf/13_243135_a_food_allergy_web_508.pdf.

Change the Equation. 2016. "In a New Survey, Americans Say, 'We're Not Good at Math.'" http://changetheequation.org/press/new-survey-americans-say-"we're-not-good-math."

Chawla, Louise. 2012. "The Importance of Access to Nature for Young Children." *Early Childhood Matters* (June): 48–51.

———. 2006. "Research Methods to Investigate Significant Life Experiences: Review and Recommendations." *Environmental Education Research* 12 (3/4): 359–74.

Claessens, Amy, and Mimi Engel. 2013. "How Important Is Where You Start? Early Mathematics Knowledge and Later School Success." *Teachers College Record* 115 (6): 1–29.

Clements, Douglas H., and Julie Sarama. 2004. "Building Blocks for Early Childhood Mathematics." *Early Childhood Research Quarterly* 19: 181–89.

Colburn, Alan. 1997. "How to Make Lab Activities More Open-ended." *CSTA Journal.* Fall 1997: 4–6.

Computational Thinking with Scratch. "What Is Computational Thinking?" Accessed January 10, 2017. http://scratched.gse.harvard.edu/ct/defining.html.

Cronin-Jones, Linda L. 2000. "The Effectiveness of Schoolyards as Sites for Elementary Science Instruction." *School Science and Mathematics* 100 (4): 203–11.

Cuny, Jan, Larry Snyder, and Jeannette M. Wing. 2010. Committee for the Workshop on Computational Thinking, NAP.

DiPerna, J. C., P. L. Morgan, and P. W. Lei. 2007. Development of Early Arithmetic, Reading, and Learning Indicators for Head Start (The EARLI Project). Semi-Annual Performance Report to the U.S. Department of Health and Human Services Administration for Children and Families.

Dowdell, K., T. Gray, and K. Malone. 2011. "Nature and Its Influence on Children's Outdoor Play." *Australian Journal of Outdoor Education* 15 (2): 24.

Duncan, G. J., et al. 2007. "School Readiness and Academic Achievement." *Developmental Psychology* 43:1428–46. doi:10.1037/0012-1649.43.6.1428

Eisenberg, Nancy. 1982. *The Development of Prosocial Behavior.* New York: Academic Press.

Eisenberg, Nancy, and Paul H. Mussen. 1989. *The Roots of Prosocial Behavior in Children.* Cambridge: Cambridge University Press.

Eltgeest, J. 1985. "The Right Question at the Right Time." In *Primary Science: Taking the Plunge* by Wynne Harlen. Portsmouth, NH: Heinemann.

Eshach, H., and M. N. Fried. 2005. "Should Science Be Taught in Early Childhood?" *Journal of Science Education and Technology* 14 (3): 315–36.

Finch, Ken. 2012. "But . . . Isn't It Dangerous? Risk and Reward in Nature Play." *Ecology Global Network.* www.ecology.com/2012/07/17/risk-reward-nature-play.

Geiken, R., B. Dystra Van Meeteren, and T. Kato. 2009. "Putting the Cart before the Horse: The Role of Socio-Moral Atmosphere in an Inquiry-Based Curriculum." *Childhood Education Infancy through Early Adolescence* 85 (4): 260–63.

Ginsburg, Herbert P. 2006. "Mathematical Play and Playful Mathematics: A Guide for Early Education" from *Play = Learning: How Play Motivates and Enhances Children's Cognitive and SocialEmotional Growth,* eds., Dorothy G. Singer, Roberta Michnick Golinkoff, and Kathy Hirsh-Pasek, eds. New York: Oxford University Press.

Gutnick, A. L., M. Robb, L. Takeuchi, and J. Kotler. 2010. *Always Connected: The New Digital Media Habits of Young Children.* New York: The Joan Ganz Cooney Center at Sesame Workshop. www.joanganzcooneycenter.org/wp-content/uploads/2011/03/jgcc_alwaysconnected.pdf.

Harlen, Wynne, and Ruth Deakin Crick. 2003. "Testing and Motivation for Learning." *Assessment in Education* 10 (2): 169–207.

Harlen, Wynne. 2006. *Teaching, Learning, and Assessing Science 5–12.* Los Angeles, Sage Publications.

Herron, M.D. 1971. "The Nature of Scientific Inquiry." *The School Review* 79 (2): 171–212.

Hong, Seong B., and Mary Trepanier-Street. 2004. "Technology: A Tool for Knowledge Construction in a Reggio Emilia Inspired Teacher Education Program." *Early Childhood Education Journal* 32 (2): 87–94.

Iman, H., K. Trundle, and R. Kantor. 2010. "Understanding the Natural Sciences in a Reggio-Emilia Inspired Preschool." *Journal of Research in Science Teaching* 47 (10): 1186–1208.

"Insect Repellent Use & Safety." 2015. www.cdc.gov/westnile/faq/repellent.html.

Joe, E. and J. Davis. 2009. "Parental Influence, School Readiness and Early Academic Achievement of African American Boys." *The Review* 17 (1): 1–61.

Kahn, P. H. 1997. "Developmental Psychology and the Biophilia Hypothesis: Children's Affiliation with Nature." *Developmental Review* 17 (1): 1–61.

Kahn, P. H., and S. R. Kellert. 2002. *Children and Nature: Psychological, Sociocultural, and Evolutionary Investigations.* Cambridge, MA: Massachusetts Institute of Technology.

Katehi, Linda, Greg Pearson, and Michael A. Feder. 2009. *Engineering in K–12 education; understanding the status and improving the prospects.* Washington, D.C.: The National Academies Press.

Kuo, Frances E., and Andrea Faber Taylor. 2004. "A Potential Natural Treatment for Attention-Deficit/Hyperactivity Disorder: Evidence from a National Study." *American Journal of Public Health* 94 (9): 1580–86.

Louv, Richard. 2005. *Last Child in the Woods: Saving Our Children from Nature-Deficit Disorder.* New York: Algonquin Press.

Martens, Mary Lee. 1999. "Productive Questions: Tools for Supporting Constructivist Learning." www.upcyclecrc.org/uploads/1/2/8/5/12859669/productivequestionsbymartensscienceandchildren5-1999.pdf.

Maxwell, L., M. Mitchell, and G. Evans. 2008. "Effects of Play Equipment and Loose Parts on Preschool Children's Outdoor Play Behavior: An Observational Study and Design Intervention." *Children, Youth and Environments* 18 (2): 36–63.

McCoach, D. B., A. A. O'Connell, and H. Levitt. 2006. "Ability Grouping across Kindergarten Using an Early Childhood Longitudinal Study." *Journal of Educational Research* 99 (6): 339–46.

McIntyre, C. L., A. H. Sheetz, C. R. Carroll, and M. C. Young. 2005. "Administration of Epinephrine for Life-Threatening Allergic Reactions in School Settings." *Pediatrics.* 116 (5): 1134–40.

Mussen, Paul Henry, and Nancy Eisenberg. 1978. *Roots of Caring, Sharing, and Helping: The Development of Prosocial Behavior in Children.* San Francisco: W. H. Freeman.

National Academy of Engineering and National Research Council. 2009. *Engineering in K–12 Education: Understanding the Status and Improving the Prospects.* Washington, DC: National Academies Press. doi:10.17226/12635.

National Association for the Education of Young Children (NAEYC). 2012. *The Common Core State Standards: Caution and Opportunity for Early Childhood Education.* Washington, DC: National Association for the Education of Young Children.

National Association for the Education of Young Children (NAEYC) and the Fred Rogers Center for Early Learning and Children's Media at Saint Vincent College. 2012. "Technology and Interactive Media as Tools in Early Childhood Programs Serving Children from Birth through Age 8." www.naeyc.org/files/naeyc/PS_technology_WEB.pdf.

National Association for Media Literacy Education. "Core Principles of Media Literacy Education in the United States." Accessed January 10, 2017. https://namle.net/publications/core-principles.

National Council of Teachers of Mathematics. 2000. *Principles and Standards for School Mathematics.* www.nctm.org/Standards-and-Positions/Principles-and-Standards/Process.

National Research Council. 2001. *Adding It Up: Helping Children Learn Mathematics.* Washington, DC: National Academies Press.

———. 2009. *Mathematics Learning in Early Childhood: Paths toward Excellence and Equity.* Washington, DC: National Academies Press.

———. 2010. *Report of a Workshop on the Scope and Nature of Computational Thinking.* Washington, DC: National Academies Press.

Next Generation Science Standards. "Development Overview." Accessed January 10, 2017. www.nextgenscience.org/development-overview.

NGSS@NSTA. 2013. "Crosscutting Concepts." http://ngss.nsta.org/CrosscuttingConceptsFull.aspx.

North American Association for Environmental Education. 2010. *Guidelines for Excellence: Early Childhood EE Programs.* Washington, DC: NAAEE Publications.

Phillips, Deborah A., Jack P. Shonkoff, eds. 2000. From Neurons to Neighborhoods: The Science of Early Childhood Development. Washington, DC: National Academies Press.

Pocketgamer.biz. 2017. "App Submissions by Month." Accessed January 4, 2017. www.pocketgamer.biz.

Reardon, Sean F. 2011. In *Whither Opportunity? Rising Inequality, Schools, and Children's Life Chances*, ed. R. Murnane and G. Duncan. New York: Russell Sage Foundation.

Robson, Sue, and Victoria Rowe. 2012. "Observing Young Children's Creative Thinking: Engageent, Involvement and Persistence." *International Journal of Early Years Education* 20 (4): 349–64.

Roe, J., and P. Aspinall. 2011. "The Restorative Outcomes of Forest School and Conventional School in Young People with Good and Poor Behaviour." *Urban Forestry & Urban Greening* 10 (3): 205–212.

———. 2012. "Adolescents' Daily Activities and the Restorative Niches that Support Them." *International Journal of Environmental Research and Public Health* 9 (9): 3227–44.

Roe, J., P. Aspinall, and C. T. Ward. 2016. "Understanding Relationships between Health, Ethnicity, Place and the Role of Urban Green Space in Deprived Urban Communities." *International Journal of Environmental Research and Public Health* 13 (7): 681.

Schwab, Joseph J. 1962. "The Teaching of Science as Enquiry." In *The Teaching of Science*. Cambridge, MA: Harvard University Press.

Selly, Patty Born. 2012. *Early Childhood Activities for a Greener Earth*. St. Paul, MN: Redleaf Press.

"SunWise." 2017. National Environmental Education Foundation. www.neefusa.org /sunwise.

U.S. Census Bureau. 2012. "Income, Poverty, and Health Insurance Coverage in the United States." *Current Population Reports*. September.

Van Meeteren, Beth, and Betty Zan. 2010. "Revealing the Work of Young Engineers in Early Childhood Education." Paper presented at the SEED (STEM in Early Education and Development) Conference, Cedar Falls, IA, May.

Wells, Nancy M., and Kristi S. Lekies. 2006. "Nature and the Life Course: Pathways from Childhood Nature Experiences to Adult Environmentalism." *Children, Youth and Environments* 16 (1): 1–24.

Wilson, Edward O. 1986. *Biophilia*. Cambridge, MA: Harvard University Press.

Wu, Q., P. Lei, J. C. DiPerna, P. Morgan, and E. Reid. 2015. "Identifying Differences in Early Mathematical Skills among Children in Head Start." *International Journal of Science and Mathematics Education* 13 (6): 1403–23.

Zamani, Zahra, and Robin Moore. 2013. "The Cognitive Play Behavior Affordances of Natural and Manufactured Elements within Outdoor Preschool Settings." *Landscape Research* 1.